BEYOND TOURISM

A Practical Guide to Meaningful Educational Travel

Kenneth Cushner

ScarecrowEducation
Lanham, Maryland • Toronto • Oxford
2004

Published in the United States of America
by ScarecrowEducation
An imprint of The Rowman & Littlefield Publishing Group, Inc.
4501 Forbes Boulevard, Suite 200, Lanham, Maryland 20706
www.scarecroweducation.com

PO Box 317
Oxford
OX2 9RU, UK

Copyright © 2004 by Kenneth Cushner

All rights reserved. No part of this publication may be reproduced, stored in a retrieval system, or transmitted in any form or by any means, electronic, mechanical, photocopying, recording, or otherwise, without the prior permission of the publisher.

British Library Cataloguing in Publication Information Available

Library of Congress Cataloging-in-Publication Data

Cushner, Kenneth.
  Beyond tourism : a practical guide to meaningful educational travel / Kenneth Cushner.
      p. cm.
  Includes bibliographical references (p.   ).
  ISBN 1-57886-154-3 (pbk. : alk. paper)
  1. Tourism. 2. Travel. 3. Students—Travel. I. Title.
  G155.A1C872 2004
  910—dc22
                                                           2004003438

∞™ The paper used in this publication meets the minimum requirements of American National Standard for Information Sciences—Permanence of Paper for Printed Library Materials, ANSI/NISO Z39.48-1992.
Manufactured in the United States of America.

To Hyla, with love.

I couldn't have gone down this road without you.
Thanks for making it a joyful and meaningful ride.

CONTENTS

1	Teacher as Traveler—Travel as Teacher	1
2	Get Ready, Get Set—Before You Go	13
3	Traveling with Class: The Trip Begins	27
4	The Power of Travel Occurs Off the Beaten Track	37
5	Learning to Travel Is Learning to See: Developing Intercultural Sensitivity	45
6	Change Your Latitude, Change Your Attitude: Facilitating Adolescent Adjustment	61
7	Learning to Live Together: Bridging Intercultural Boundaries with Youth Dialogue	81
8	The Making of World-Class Teachers: International Student Teaching	99
9	Beyond Tourism: The Importance of Experience on Impact	111
10	Building Trust, Relationships, and Commitment, Even Though Sometimes Things Go Wrong	123

| 11 | Making It Work for You: Travel Tips and Resources | 145 |

References 159

Index 163

About the Author 165

1

TEACHER AS TRAVELER—
TRAVEL AS TEACHER

Do not go where the path may lead; go instead where there is no path and leave a trail.

—Ralph Waldo Emerson

When I was young, I wanted to be a game warden. Thank Joy and George Adamson for that one. Ever since I read of their experiences raising Elsa the lioness in their books *Born Free* and *Living Free*, I envisioned myself working in the bush, saving and protecting vulnerable wildlife, helping to raise and teach the young, and then setting them free to encounter the world on their own. During my undergraduate college years, I must have written to more than forty different game parks throughout Africa—from Kenya to South Africa—seeking work of almost any kind. I even studied Kiswahili, the language spoken throughout East Africa, as my undergraduate foreign language requirement. At the time, I was the only student to have taken the full two-year cycle of Kiswahili, learning from Meki, my teacher and mentor, who had come from Tanzania to Ohio to pursue his Ph.D. Talk about assumptions and stereotypes. The bureaucracy of the African Studies Department at the time assumed I was an African American student. Every six months I would receive a postcard reminding me that it was time to get my blood checked for sickle-cell anemia.

But I'm white and Jewish and not a likely candidate for sickle-cell anemia. And inexperienced game wardens weren't particularly needed, especially at a time when most African countries were busy nationalizing themselves and struggling to dispose of any reminders of their colonial past. So I became a teacher instead. I can barely recall any of the Kiswahili I learned, except for a few fun tongue twisters Meki had taught me. Try this: *Nne na nne ni nane.* It means "four plus four equals eight"—kind of handy for me as a teacher. Next, try this one: *Nyanya nyangu ana nyanya nyingi.* You'd never guess that it means "My grandmother has many tomatoes," with *nyanya* meaning both "tomatoes" and "grandmother." The context, obviously, is critical here, as it is in most cross-cultural encounters. While the phrase isn't too handy anymore, I used to enjoy teaching it to my friends. A longtime friend of mine, Jim, recently tried it out on a Kenyan taxi driver in Las Vegas. It got him nowhere, either because it's an inaccurate translation or he didn't quite get the pronunciation right. Try it yourself: *Nyanya nyangu ana nyanya nyingi.* It's fun, anyway.

Most teachers do for children many of the things the Adamsons did for the young, vulnerable, and orphaned animals they nurtured and returned to the natural habitat. Teachers are entrusted with helping raise the young of our species by providing them with some of the specialized skills, guidance, nurturance, support, and experiences that might "set them free," so to speak, to become functional adult members of the species, ready to face a complex society comprising our own producers and consumers, predators and prey, vultures and other scavengers, and general dog-eat-dog world. And like the Adamsons, most teachers help others in many ways that neither they, nor those on whose behalf they are working, could ever imagine.

Opening up new horizons for others comes naturally to all good teachers. Today, if young people are to be adequately prepared for the future, these horizons must include the broader world in which teachers and their students live. Time and again we are reminded of the multifaceted, changing, and interconnected nature of our world. This was brought home to us most recently with the horrific events that unfolded in the United States on September 11, 2001. The tragedies that occurred on that day reached far beyond the borders of any one nation—instantly uniting people from more than seventy countries that lost citizens and were otherwise directly impacted by this disaster. The events that have unfolded in the aftermath of that incident continue to demonstrate how our world has changed, how interconnected and vulnerable we all are, and how little most of us really know about others around the globe.

To continue to teach from a relatively narrowly focused or traditional orientation will do little to move us forward as individuals, as a nation, or as a world. Like it or not, education is a global concern, and we are remiss if we do not educate all of our students to be competent, global citizens who not only understand others but also possess the skills and dispositions required to collaborate to solve some of the world's complicated problems. The problems faced by citizens of the world today are so complex and interconnected that they will only be solved by the concerted collaborative efforts of many people from a variety of backgrounds—or they will not be solved.

Teachers are also futurists. That is, they must project the future needs of their students as well as society and, with that in mind, develop educational experiences that achieve the goals and objectives determined to be of most need. But teachers must themselves be citizens of the world if they are to guide their students in this direction. If teachers do not reach out across the cultural divide and learn how to bridge gaps, if they do not consider their global citizenry, and if they do not take their own risks, then it will not be possible to adequately prepare young students with the kinds of skills they will need in order to be born free in the twenty-first century. Teachers, thus, are central to the process of intercultural development and must model such an orientation for their young students as well as for their communities.

An overriding objective of this book is to inspire others, both educators and noneducators, to include international as well as domestic intercultural encounters as an increasing part of the education of young people. In no other time in human history has it been more essential that individuals develop a global or intercultural perspective and reach a certain level of comfort in their intercultural interactions. Not only is it necessary that individuals develop this broader understanding of the world, but it is also becoming increasingly possible to do so. Through sensitive and well-designed experiences, students can move along the continuum of intercultural development from a state of ethnocentrism to one that is more ethnorelative; from being rather inexperienced in terms of intercultural sensitivity and competence to being able to think more broadly and interact more effectively with people different from oneself.

Essential to this development are the influential, firsthand, interpersonal encounters that travel brings and that serve to make many of the abstract concepts of intercultural understanding practical and real. This book, thus, is part autobiography of a traveling teacher and teacher educator, part travelogue, part lessons learned, and part guidelines for those interested in developing meaningful group travel experiences or who are simply interested in getting the most that they can from traveling with groups. I welcome you on this journey.

Travel, while enriching, engaging, and educational for the individual or group, is rarely easy. Educators committed to developing and delivering thoughtful curricular experiences designed to achieve certain goals and objectives related to travel and intercultural learning must understand the reasons people travel, as well as the obstacles that may be encountered.

It is interesting to consider that the derivation of the word *travel* is from the word *travail*. Its root, however, is ironically from the Latin *tripalium*, referring to a medieval torture rack. It implies bodily or mental labor; toil, especially of a painful or oppressive nature; exertion; hardship; suffering; a journey. A surprising relationship perhaps, yet similar to how some people may recall their years of schooling. And as many have experienced, and Cosineau (1998) reminds us, when traveling, there are moments that are difficult and demanding—perhaps like being "on the rack." It is a bit surprising, but people often recall the more difficult and demanding moments of their travels: the times they were sick, got lost, had something stolen, or met a shifty local. Yet, people tend to feel a sense of accomplishment and pride when they report that they have "survived" the ordeal. This may appear a peculiar and non-commonsense finding, but it seems to be a rather common part of the process.

With preparation and guidance, the challenging and difficult moments of travel can be reduced, eliminated, or at least managed and used as a point of learning. But caution is needed. Some would say we are fortunate today because the modern travel industry has removed much of the risk and difficulty from traveling. Although much of group travel can be protected and somewhat sanitized, it really is only through direct personal encounters that true cultural learning can occur. Nevertheless, whether we are on vacation, traveling with students, or on our own far-reaching adventure, we can look at the demands along the road as either torment or opportunities to stretch and grow.

We might ask, "Why do people continue to invest an incredible amount of time and money to move themselves and their belongings over vast distances, uprooting themselves from the surroundings they have become accustomed to, and exposing themselves to potential dangers and certain discomforts?" Obviously there are many reasons people travel, some of which are personal, some of which are for one's livelihood, and some of which are involuntary, as with refugees from war-torn regions of the world.

Increasingly, the business community demands continual movement of people, goods, and services. Accounting for much of the travel people do today, the business executive can move with relative ease between the cultures of the world's multinational and international corporations. The United States alone serves as home to well over 6,000 international firms, while an equally high number of American corporations have offices overseas. Globalization of the world's industries represents a significant amount of the world travel today. This is one of the reasons young people should learn the art of travel—many will eventually join a global workforce.

For many, travel represents a vacation or an opportunity to experience something different in another part of the world. For others it has become a hobby, and in this day of excesses and expendable income, they travel the world collecting passport stamps as stamp collectors accumulate philatelic mementos, or as any other hobbyist amasses the artifacts of his or her pastime. Travel in this sense provides an escape from one's daily routines by offering relaxation and possibly fresh, albeit brief, encounters and new experiences that could not be found at home. It is projected that the travel industry will be the largest worldwide industry within the coming decade, fueled, in large part, by this type of recreational traveler. This is another reason young people should learn the art of travel—as numbers of travelers increase, it is important that students become good stewards of the Earth and its people in order to learn how to travel responsibly and in a sustainable or ecologically sound manner.

With increased internationalization and globalization we have witnessed a homogenization of much of the travel experience. For many people, travel consists of taxi rides between rather similar international airports and familiar, and comfortable, brand-name and chain hotels. Many find themselves so uncomfortable when they are out of their familiar surroundings that they become critical of the local's way of life, and the travel industry has gone to incredible lengths to provide such travelers with accommodations that, behind the facade of difference, are designed either to replicate what one would find at home or to mask the reality of where one is. Some have reminded us that when you travel, keep in mind that a foreign country is not designed to make you comfortable. It is designed to make its own people comfortable. For travelers of this type, who typically want the comforts of home, it may not matter where they are—just that they are somewhere else enjoying that to which they have become accustomed. They don't really want things to be different; they just want them to be elsewhere. Herein lies another reason we should teach the art of travel—to help people learn to see beyond their own frame of reference and to welcome the differences they will encounter in the world.

Some people may travel to avoid an uncomfortable problem or situation at home—to escape from a bad marriage, a stifling career, or dissatisfaction with oneself, only to find that the problem cannot be avoided and that it accompanies the traveler. Being away from one's familiar context and support groups then exacerbates the problem the person tried to avoid in the first place. One soon finds that it is easier to change one's surroundings than it is to change one's heart. There is a truism here. No matter where you go, you, too, will be there. You simply cannot escape yourself. Herein lies another reason to teach the art of travel—to help people understand what it can and cannot accomplish.

Still others argue that travel is in our nature, and that people really have no choice but to be constantly on the move. The hunting and gathering way of life, they contend, is what is natural for humans; it is hardwired into our systems, and if fully embraced, it would guarantee the sustainability of the planet. In his book *Ishmael*, Daniel Quinn proposes that the invention of agriculture marked the beginning of the environmental decline. He argues that some 12,000 years ago, when people stopped wandering and became relatively stationary, they assumed the role of God by determining which species of plants and animals lived and which would not be tolerated on land they designated as cropland. We have witnessed an increase in the number of extinct and endangered species, as well as global threats of pollution, ever since we became stationary and stopped our hunting and gathering ways.

One can find evidence of the tensions that might have developed in our evolutionary past if we listen to the words or observe the behavior of some of the world's indigenous people. A Caribou Eskimo, for instance, once said to Dr. Knud Rassmussen, "What can we do? We were born with the Great Unrest. Our father taught us that life is one long journey on which only the unfit are left behind" (Chatwin 1987). Or, in Turi's *Book of Lappland*, we learn that Sami consider themselves to have the same nature as reindeer: in the springtime they long for the mountains; in the winter they long for the woods. Chatwin (1987) has noted the strong need for human mobility. Day in and day out, he says, a baby cannot be walked enough. He suggests that if babies instinctively demand to be walked, the mother on the African savanna must have been walking too: from camp to camp on her daily foraging round, to the water hole, and on visits to neighbors. Evolutionary evidence does exist to support this contention. Recent research suggests that it may not have been the development of tools that prompted early humans to venture out of Africa, as first believed. Rather, simple wanderlust may have been part of *Homo erectus*'s personality, encouraging it to change its range and habitat—perhaps in pursuit of game (Lemonick 2000).

One might even trace the human drive for movement to others in the animal kingdom. In *The Descent of Man*, Darwin (Chatwin 1987) points out that in certain species of birds, the migratory impulse is stronger than the maternal instinct. He cites the example of Audubon's goose, which, deprived of its pinion feathers, started out to walk the journey on foot. Or of the mother that would abandon her offspring in the nest rather than miss her scheduled long journey south. He then goes on to describe the sufferings of a bird, penned up at the season of its migration, that would flail its wings and bloody its breast against the bars of its cage.

To counter this, some Western psychiatrists, politicians, and tyrants have tried to convince us that the wandering life is an aberrant form of behavior; a neurosis; a form of unfulfilled sexual longing; a sickness that, in the interests of civilization, must be suppressed (Chatwin 1987). Nazi propagandists, for instance, claimed that Rom (Gypsies) and Jews—people they assumed to have wandering in their genes—could find no place in a stable Reich. They, thus, became the target of persecution, as they were thought to be different.

Yet in the East, people still preserve the once-universal concept that wandering reestablishes the original harmony that once existed between humans and the universe. For some, travel provides answers to questions they cannot find at home. *Solvitur ambulando*, it has been said—"it is solved by walking." And Gautama Buddha's last words to his disciples were, "Walk on!"

But perhaps not all of the answers to one's questions may be found on the road. One must consider carefully that some people travel the world over in search of what they need, only to find it at the home they had left. Perhaps internal travel, as in meditation, prayer, and other forms of introspection, is a more fruitful means to satisfy one's desires and needs in this realm.

Finally, some people travel as a means not only to learn, but also to teach—to help open up worlds for others that they might not readily find by themselves. Before the development of tourism, travel was conceived of as a form of study, and its fruits were considered to be the adornment of the mind and the formation of judgment (Fussell 1987). The traveler was a student of what he or she sought. In such a case, travel can be accompanied by intellectual or spiritual growth; a sense of connectedness with something greater than oneself and one's immediate surroundings—be that nature, people, or both. Read of the first travel excursion I made with students and decide for yourself which, if any, of these outcomes were realized.

> It was beginning to get colder and windier, the rain was picking up, and there I was one night, searching the island for a fifteen-year-old student who, at the moment, was missing and nowhere to be found. Who would have thought that just three months after graduating from college and beginning a career in teaching, I would be traveling to Greece and worrying about losing a student?
>
> Most of my peers were in the United States, teaching in schools quite similar to those they had gone through themselves. And most of them wanted nothing more than to return to their home community and teach in their alma mater, as many young teachers, unfortunately, still desire to-

day. Not me. I didn't even have a passion for teaching when I first went to college. I disliked my own school experience so much that returning to the classroom as a teacher was absolutely the last thing I ever thought I would do. Then I found myself at the American School in Zurich doing my student teaching. It was there that I discovered what an education might really be. This school was an exciting, engaging environment that young people wanted to be part of—as did I. Perhaps, I thought, I could be a different kind of teacher; one who would create an environment where young people wanted to be. Teaching, for me, as I was soon to find out, would become a way to learn and to expand my horizons as well as those of my students.

I had been in my first official teaching job for no more than three months when I embarked on a rather ambitious adventure. Having just completed my student teaching, and remaining on staff teaching biology on a part-time basis, I wanted to see as much of the world as possible. Not really having the necessary resources to fund such escapades, I looked to my students, and their supportive parents, for the opportunity. Perhaps—just perhaps—I could recruit a large enough group of students who would be interested in traveling to Greece over our spring break that I could cover my expenses. It seemed worth the effort.

To my surprise, fourteen students and their parents expressed interest—and more surprising, trust. The parents allowed me to take their children, most of them between the ages of fourteen and seventeen, by train from Zurich to the port town of Brindisi, tucked away in the heel of Italy's boot. From there we would catch an overnight ferry to Greece and spend the better part of two weeks traveling between Athens and the islands. Now, this was not going to be first-class travel by any stretch of the imagination. We would be traveling like most student backpackers—staying in youth hostels, using public transportation in and around Athens, and traveling third-class by ship between the islands of the Aegean wherever possible. That was the only way I knew how to travel, having Arthur Frommer's "five dollars a day" as a mantra in my ear. Any "real" traveler, I thought, had to remain within such a budget, and I would guide my students with this strategy. The highlight of our trip would be a one-week stay on the island of Santorini, or Thíra, as it is known locally, in five homes that I was able to rent through a travel agent in Zurich.

It was not easy traveling to Santorini, but it was an adventure for each of us on many levels. My young students were surprisingly comfortable carrying their belongings in backpacks, staying in inexpensive student-oriented accommodations, and sailing south to Crete, where we stayed for three days studying the ancient Minoan civilization. A short four-hour, but very choppy, ferry ride on stormy seas took us north to Santorini. I never expected to meet so many locals on such a brief trip, but I seemed to be the only one who had any seasickness remedies on hand. Suddenly the most popular person on the ship, I passed out pill after pill of Dramamine as we swayed from side to side, clutching our bags out of fear that they might fly overboard and our bellies as they, for many, were relieved overboard. Half of the ship was ill by the time we arrived in the tranquil port—and I was out of Dramamine.

Some believe the island of Santorini to be the legendary Atlantis, blown apart by the volcanic eruption some 4,000 years ago that sent a tidal wave rushing to destroy the Minoan civilization in Crete. Today, where once was a large circular island, the only habitable portion is a crescent-shaped ridge that rises some 1,000 feet from the water a few hundred meters from the still-active volcanic cone. Ships enter through a channel, with the volcanic cone on one side and the remaining landmass on the other, and passengers can see the sparkling white buildings atop the island that characterize many popular photos of the Greek Islands. One could, at the time of our venture, reach the villages only by taking a burro or walking up more than 800 broad zigzag steps from the "old" port to the town of Thíra on the top of the island. Today, as the world of travel continues to change, a cable car whisks visitors from the port to the top with little effort.

Our homes were well situated, about one-half kilometer from the center of town, making it easy to get around. It was a safe community, and after our daily excursions to archaeological ruins and volcanic sites, and general jaunts around the island, I felt comfortable allowing the students to explore on their own.

This was my first exposure to Greek folk traditions, as it was for my students. Night after night we would find ourselves in local restaurants, cafés, and nightclubs to observe, and ultimately participate in, local song and folk dance. This was also my introduction to the tradition of men dancing with other men—something quite foreign to me at the time. While initially reluctant, I soon learned to join in the fun and began to look forward to those evenings. Besides, how could I expect my students to welcome new experiences if I was reluctant to do the same?

We were welcomed wherever we went—in small villages, in people's homes, in their churches, and, of course, in their shops. Greeks by their nature are quite open to outsiders, more so than they may be to other Greek nationals to whom they are not related. Many visitors to Greece quickly find themselves included in the in-group and leave the country with fond memories of the warmth and hospitality of its people. Why should I have worried about the evenings? Where could my students go? The entire island encompassed twenty-nine square miles and was populated by fewer than 500 people. But there I was, worrying, not only about the one student that night, but also about my entire teaching career. Why travel in the first place? What was I doing here? What brought me to this point? The questions never seemed to end.

About ten o'clock that night, about five days into our stay on Santorini and toward the end of our trip, I was making the rounds between the houses to check that everyone was accounted for. I came up one student short, and after rechecking all the houses, I was certain that Irene was missing. Irene, a rather quiet girl of fifteen who had been a pleasant, but somewhat detached, participant, was not someone I would expect to worry over. Nevertheless, I *was* worried and really did not know where to begin. I was especially concerned because the weather had been getting worse as the night progressed. I called together the other two chaperones and we planned our strategy. Linda would head toward town—perhaps Irene was in one of the nightclubs or cafés. I would head toward the waterfront, and Barb would stay near the homes in case Irene returned.

It was getting windier by the hour, and it was pretty evident that a storm was approaching. By the time I started out, the gusts of wind were so strong that the branches of the few trees that remained on the island appeared as if they would be gone by morning. I walked through the wind and down the 800 zigzag steps toward the port area in search of Irene. Where could she be? What could have happened to her? I didn't know, nor did I really know where I was going, but I had to do something. A myriad of possibilities floated through my mind, none of which I really wanted to entertain at the moment.

As I reached the waterfront I noticed a form hunched over in the darkness. There, all alone, was Irene, sitting crouched over on the pier with her head hung between her hands. She was cold, wet, and bawling her eyes out. I approached, anxious and cautious but quite relieved to have found her.

What the problem was, I couldn't have guessed. And it wasn't forthcoming—at least not at first. We walked back the long way up the steps and toward our houses, initially in silence. I wasn't quite sure what to say to a crying young girl, but I had to know what had happened and what had brought her to tears. Breaking the awkward silence, I simply asked, "What happened?"

"I was going to go with him . . . I wanted to be with him," she blurted out between tears.

"Go with who?" I asked. "Be with who?" It seems that Irene had met a Greek sailor earlier in the day and, as she put it, had fallen in love. She told me that she had thought seriously about joining her new friend and running away with him! A fifteen-year-old in love with one day's meeting? Was it possible, even without a working knowledge of the other's language? I decided, at least for the moment, that was a reality I had to accept.

Now I really began to worry. Here I was, a new teacher having just begun my career. Irene had supposedly fallen in love with someone she had just met earlier in the day. What had transpired throughout the day I did not know, but I instinctively began to count the months. If anything had happened and she became pregnant, she, her parents, and the school administration would know in about, say, three to four months. The school year would be over and I would have returned to the States. If she was pregnant was I liable? Would this end my teaching career? The possibilities were endless as I waited, and waited, and worried . . .

Fortunately for all, Irene did not become pregnant, and I am still teaching. And while, at times, the travel experience did seem torturous, at least emotionally for me as well as Irene, we all learned a tremendous amount as a result of the trip. Aside from concrete experiences interacting with present-day Greek society, touring through early Greek ruins, and studying ancient Minoan civilization, the students developed a sense of independence and group identification that could not have been achieved in the traditional classroom. And I learned that group travel with students, while stressful at times, has a much bigger payoff than most anything else a teacher might do in school. What better way is there to learn to trust oneself and one another, as well as others in the world? In travel, teacher and student go forward, ideally with open arms and an open mind, to embrace the world. Young people can be trusted to be conscientious members of a traveling group, and can take responsibility and look out for others. This was something I was certain I would be doing more of in the future.

❷

GET READY, GET SET—
BEFORE YOU GO

The day on which one starts out is not the day to start preparation.

—Nigerian Folk Saying

"**Do** you know what I think I'll have a really hard time with?" Maria reflected during the debriefing session. "When you men have to blow your nose, you walk over to the water's edge, block a nostril, exhale really hard toward the water, repeat the procedure with your other nostril, wipe your nose with your hand, and then rinse your hand off in the water. UGH! How disgusting!"

"And do you know what really bothers me about you Americans?" was the quick reply. "When you have to blow your nose, you pull a handkerchief or tissue out of your pocket or purse, blow your nose into it, roll it up in a ball, and then put it back and carry it around with you for the rest of the day. And some of you then go and wash the handkerchief with your other clothes. UGH! How disgusting!"

Good teachers are constantly on the lookout for the teachable moment, and Maria's reaction presented an invaluable opportunity to discuss and learn about the concept of ethnorelativity. What appears to be healthy and appropriate from one perspective may be seen as dirty and disgusting from another. Cordial and formal through one person's eyes becomes cold and stuffy through another's. Tactful and polite can seem overbearing and insincere.

People, both as individuals and as groups, are conditioned to see the world from a particular point of view. Others' perspectives, beliefs, points of view, and ways of doing things are, as a result, often seen as suspect, inferior, or just plain wrong. For the most part, people do not embrace such an attitude out of maliciousness. Rather, it is a consequence of the ethnocentrism that people adopt as a means of protecting their own worldview and the considerable amount of time and energy they have invested to understand and maintain that reality. After all, one of the main purposes of culture is to pass on to the next generation those aspects that are deemed important. Ethnocentrism, or the tendency to view the world and evaluate others from one's own perspective, thus becomes an important element of group survival. It can also become an obstacle to the attainment of an ethnorelative orientation and intercultural sensitivity.

Greg Trifonovitch, a former intercultural specialist at the East-West Center in Honolulu, spent many years preparing American teachers and administrators, like Maria, to assume visiting teaching assignments in the South Pacific. Constructing a simulated South Pacific village setting on about twenty-five acres on the Hawaiian island of Moloka'i, Greg would invite groups of would-be teachers, administrators, and their families for two-week orientation experiences. Here, in the safety of this constructed environment, Maria and others like her would have the opportunity to sample a bit of what life might be like for them once they arrived at their final destination, be it the islands of Tuvalu, Kapingamarangi, or Kwajalein, or any of the better-known islands scattered throughout the South Pacific.

Accompanying the new recruits would be a number of Pacific Islanders who would serve as trainers and consultants and help to create a simulated yet "authentic" island setting. For the first week, the trainers would speak only in their native language, thus adding to the range of factors to which the trainees had to adjust. In such a setting, people like Maria could project themselves into the future and, if they felt that the subsequent real-world adjustment in the Pacific would be too difficult, decide to remove themselves from the project before they made a significant overseas transition.

People would voice a range of worries and concerns in the debriefing that followed the orientation experience. It was during one such debriefing exchange that Maria's reaction to nose-blowing was discussed. Some asked, Would there be flush toilets once they got out to their island? They were told, rather matter-of-factly, "Yes, about every six hours the tide comes in, and every six hours the tide goes out again." At least one doesn't have to clean toilets on a regular basis.

People would also practice gathering food resources as many of the locals might do. They soon found that it was rather time consuming, and quite difficult by the way, to gather coconuts from palm trees, break into them without destroying much of the contents, and fish from the local waters to gather enough sustenance for just one meal. After a few days, participants would discuss what it might be like to eat the village dog, a frequent visitor in the village site. People soon discovered the first of many disconfirmed expectations—that paradise may not be the idyllic place it is made out to be, and that life may be more challenging for some than anticipated. Perhaps this was the forerunner of the popular *Survivor* television series; and a perfect example of Darwin's "survival of the fittest."

Information taken for granted and perceived one way in one cultural context may have a significantly different meaning in another. The technical term for this is categorization. It is a psychological process that enables people to simplify the world around them by grouping similar items together. Culture teaches people how to categorize the world.

Stop for a moment and consider the relatively simple example of the common dog. In the United States, as in many countries of the West, the dog is thought of as a member of the family, "man's best friend," some would say, and may be found eating in the kitchen, sitting on the couch or bed, and even donning a sweater if going for a walk in the cold night air. From a traditional Muslim perspective, the dog may be viewed as an animal to be avoided at all costs—as many Westerners would classify a rather lowly animal such as a rat or pig. In yet other parts of the world, particularly in some parts of Southeast Asia or the South Pacific, dog may be considered an important and preferred part of one's diet and be eaten—not eating—in the kitchen.

There is nothing inherently right or wrong about any of these practices; it is simply that one's culture has exerted such pressure on its members that most don't even consider the possibility that alternative ways of thinking can exist. What is wrong and quite problematic for those engaged in intercultural interactions are the negative judgments or attributions that are often made about those who do things in a different manner. Thus, some consider the dog-eater cruel and barbaric—"How could that disgusting person eat my dog?" Therein lies one of the dangers of ethnocentrism: people have a tendency to judge others, not only in a negative manner, but also as inferior, simply because they operate from a different cultural context and view life from their own culture's point of view.

But understanding and accommodating these differences are two distinct skills that cannot be accomplished nor sufficiently achieved from a cognitive-only approach to learning. Literally thousands of good books have been written, hundreds of films and videos have been produced, and countless effective speakers can present hours of relevant and interesting information about culture and intercultural contact. Unfortunately, the link between simply having knowledge and subsequently feeling different about others or behaving more effectively in a cross-cultural situation is weak at best. People really must have significant, firsthand intercultural experiences, as travel provides or as Greg's simulated cross-cultural encounters illustrate, if they are to become truly functional in a cross-cultural setting.

There may be nothing more critical to a successful international or intercultural encounter than preparing oneself and others for the experience one is about to embark upon. For the solo traveler who is off on her or his own adventure this may mean gathering maps, guidebooks, lists of possible accommodations and means of travel, and so forth. When organizing travel where the major purpose is the development of cross-cultural sensitivity or the attainment of an international or intercultural perspective, in addition to the nuts and bolts of daily living, one must focus attention on such things as cross-cultural differences in communication, behavior, attitudes, and values.

When working with groups or educational programs, one must point out for participants the processes involved in culture learning: understanding themselves as cultural beings; becoming less ethnocentric in their orientation; unlearning some of what they have spent their entire lives learning; and then relearning new knowledge, insights, and skills that will enable them to function effectively with a new mind-set and within a new context.

A comprehensive orientation program prior to an international experience can provide an opportunity for people to engage in culture learning while considering how they might respond and react in a new setting. The skilled and artful teacher or cross-cultural trainer thus is more a creator or an engineer, constructing an environment with forethought in such a manner that a particularly desired outcome is achieved and has real meaning for the learner. Overcoming ethnocentrism and one's own prejudices becomes one of the critical dimensions of this effort.

Young students often enjoy writing to, or now e-mailing, young people in other countries. Teachers can involve their students in this activity on a regular basis as one way to integrate social studies and language arts while building upon and sharing with them the teacher's own international experiences. Early in my teaching career my students were engaged in writing to pen pals as part of integrated language arts and social studies activities. Each week, students would write letters to other young people around the world describing their way of life and inquiring about such issues as the daily activities of children, the environment, local culture and cultural conflict, and global news events that could be examined from different perspectives. And each week they would anxiously await the mail, anticipating replies from around the world. They regularly wrote to students in such countries as the Soviet Union (this was pre-perestroika), Liberia, Japan, Israel, and Belize and actively exchanged photos, school artifacts, and other kid-related memorabilia.

One particularly cold February afternoon a box from our pen pals in Belize arrived that was literally overflowing with letters, stamps, stories, artwork, seashells, and a promise of larger artifacts that were to arrive in a separate mailing. In the letter from the teacher was a request that we consider hosting a small group of his students. If it was possible, he would like to bring some students to visit us during the month of June. It was our luck, and his good fortune, that because we were in a laboratory school that was affiliated with a university, we were, in fact, in session for half days from mid-June to mid-July. That was how it all began. We invited our pen pals from Belize to spend a few weeks with us. They would stay with local host families, attend school in the mornings, and participate in a number of cultural and recreational activities in the afternoons and on weekends.

It was with this in mind that James Ramos brought four young students from the village of Dangriga in the southern part of Belize to our school in northeastern Ohio. The differences between the two settings, the United States and Belize, were quite extreme. Most people know of Belize as the former British Honduras, which obtained its independence from Britain in 1964. A tiny country, it lies just east of Guatemala and south of the Yucatán Peninsula and is bordered by the Caribbean. The country, at the time, had no building taller than four stories, and hence no elevator in the nation, and only one hotel that could be booked from abroad through a standard travel agency. Belize, as has often been said, is "well off the beaten track" and, as the guidebooks continue to say, can be a dangerous place that is frequented by drug runners and others escaping the law from somewhere else.

In 1979, when this exchange began, the town of Dangriga, also known as Stann Creek, was largely a fishing village and citrus fruit processing center. Located south of the capital of Belmopan, Dangriga boasted a population of about 5,000 people, mostly of Gurifuna heritage, an ethnic group that traces its roots to Africa. Today, just over 8,000 people call Dangriga home. The village had no paved roads, a couple of dozen telephones, only a few televisions, which would, on occasion, receive broadcasts from Mexico or Guatemala (Belize had no television station of its own), and one VCR that was owned by a businessman whose brother had brought it from New York. Although the country's infrastructure has certainly developed in recent years, it remains an adventurer's delight. And Belize City still has the reputation of attracting many who are running from the law for one reason or another. Modern-day pirates, some would say.

Mr. Ramos, and his students Leroy, Nikita, Louise, and Anna, departed Dangriga for the adventure of a lifetime. It was their first trip out of the country, and they spent about fifty dollars in quarters in the Miami airport while waiting for their connecting flight to Ohio, this being their first exposure to video game technology. This really was to be an intercultural educator's delight.

Talk about assumptions and disconfirmed expectations. Not wanting to overwhelm the children with a large reception when they arrived in Ohio, the four host families met their students at my home the day the group arrived from Belize. Assuming that children growing up along the shores of the Caribbean would be natural swimmers, if for no other reason than because they were active in fishing, or simply for safety purposes, I encouraged the students to go for a swim in our apartment pool.

It was a good thing I went along with the kids. My students, eager to swim and having a bit of their own anxiety and excitement to burn off, began running toward the pool from quite a distance away. Throwing their towels to the side as they ran, they plunged into the water. It was a good thing no one else was around because they made quite a ruckus and would have splashed many by their antics. Nikita, Louise, Anna, and Leroy followed suit, although a bit less enthusiastically than my students. But in they went, one right after the other, laughing and frolicking about. Looking toward one end of the pool, I saw Leroy, still at the bottom, arms flailing about underwater, going nowhere. Realizing that he was not about to rise to the surface, I jumped in and lifted him up until he could breathe.

In all the excitement of the moment Leroy simply followed suit and joined the activity; perhaps he did not want to be left out, or he assumed the water was shallow, or maybe he didn't think about it at all. It seems that many Belizean children are rather afraid of the water and spend little time, if any, actually swimming in the sea. This would not be the last time we had to look out for our inexperienced visitors. Crossing busy city streets, an everyday occurrence in our culture, was another new experience to which they had to become accustomed.

My students and their families were eager to share all that they could and to spend as much time as possible with the visitors. There were constant battles over who would go home with whom, who might be able to spend the night or weekend, who was invited to dinner, and so forth. The children all seemed color-blind, and they eagerly engaged with one another in a variety of ways. We all learned a considerable amount from one another.

There was real disappointment at the end of the experience with another disconfirmed expectation. James had gone away for a weekend to visit some friends from his village who were in Detroit—or at least that is what he told me. When he hadn't returned on Sunday as planned I began to get a little worried. The following afternoon he telephoned and informed me that he would not be returning to Belize, let alone our school, as he had decided to stay in the United States and affiliate more closely with his church—they would take care of him and support his desire to study in an American college. "Oh, and by the way," he went on to tell me, "I have the students' passports that they need in order to return home next week, and I don't know how to get them back to you." Was it possible that his real purpose was to gain entry into the United States using his four students and our offer to host them as his vehicle? And this was to be a man of the cloth?

It was obvious that James had no intention of returning the passports to us. After countless telephone calls, a three-hour drive across the state to rendezvous with him, and a very cold and angry good-bye between the two of us, I retrieved the passports and returned home. The following week we said our good-byes to the children, and I accompanied them to their connecting flight in Miami. The impact on all participants—the Belizean children, my students, and their families as well—was extremely positive. This was the first of many intense international interpersonal relationships I helped develop for young people over the years.

One might ask, "Why would anyone want to travel overseas with a group of young children?" Talk about student-directed learning. My next group travel experience unfolded at the request of the students themselves.

After the children went back, unaccompanied, to Belize, my students asked, "Gee Mr. C. [it was Mr. C. then], can we go there?" Not having really thought about it, I followed up their request with a letter to parents informing them that their children had expressed an interest in going to Belize to visit their newfound friends, and if there was sufficient interest, I would pursue the possibility. To my surprise, seventeen students came back with letters from their parents saying something to the effect of, "You want to take my child to Belize for a few weeks at Christmas time? By all means, PLEASE do!" That was all I needed to hear—the kids were willing to travel, their parents were eager to send them away for two weeks, and I was off making plans.

What came as a surprise was the number of parents who expressed an interest in joining the trip. One set of parents initially signed the form thinking that we were planning to visit an inner-city school about thirty minutes away. They only understood the extent of the project and our true destination when they were later asked to cough up a one hundred dollar deposit. What was really confusing was that this very same family had been stationed in Panama—a mere 500 miles from Belize—during their years in the military and hadn't a clue where Belize was located. More evidence that our schools, and in this case the military, had failed to instill knowledge of geography in their students and trainees.

Making plans for this coming venture was not easy. As we had already discovered, there was very little tourist information available about Belize, there was only one hotel that could be booked from outside the country, and no one seemed willing to arrange group travel programs to a place labeled as a "hideout for criminals." It really was surprising that so many parents entrusted their children to me given how little we actually knew about the country. I can only assume that they knew even less than I did—but trusted me nonetheless. It was an awesome responsibility.

I wrote to numerous international social service agencies, the Peace Corps, the Usher family, whose son, Nikita, had been with us in the summer, and anyone else I could think of in an attempt to find out how to travel with a group of twenty-two people, mostly ten- to eleven-year-old children, from Ohio to Belize. Most of the replies yielded little hope, except the one from Hubert and Aura Usher, Nikita's parents. They were willing to assist and would make all the local plans for our upcoming visit, provided that we could get to the border between Mexico and Belize. They asked me to send a check for $800 that would pay for a bus to take us from the Mexican border town of Chetumal to Dangriga. The plan sounded as if it came out of some spy movie from the early 1960s and a bit fishy at first, but a certain element of trust is necessary in order to venture out into the world as a traveler. The check was sent, fingers were crossed, and plans begun. We now *had* to go, if for no other reason than to track down my money in case we were stood up.

Flying into Mérida, the capital of Yucatán, we would spend a few days visiting Mayan ruins and other local sites. With any luck, we would also spend time visiting a Mexican school. The American consulate seemed an appropriate place to begin seeking assistance. No response. No problem. A few days of organized sightseeing in the region would keep us busy and fulfilled before we departed by public bus from Mérida to Chetumal on the Mexican–Belizean border. Here we would rendezvous with our hoped-for bus and travel the remaining distance through Belize to Dangriga—assuming all went well. The plans finally came together. All that had to be done was to stay on top of things to be certain that everything was in place in time for our departure in mid-December.

Next was the task of preparing the students, none of whom had ever traveled outside the United States before, and many of whom had never been on an airplane. I really was at a loss as to how to best orient the children, as neither materials nor information was readily available to help us understand what to expect in terms of either culture or country. And because we hadn't considered traveling ourselves until after our visitors left, we never really used their expertise to prepare for a return visit.

Belize was *so* different from any of its neighboring countries, being the only English-speaking former British colony in the Spanish-speaking, Latin-oriented Central American region. I knew we would be spending a few days in Mexico and assumed, perhaps wrongly so, that many Belizeans would speak Spanish because Spanish-speaking people and nations surround them on all sides. And I knew we would encounter many surprises along the way that neither the children nor I could anticipate. Nevertheless, I wanted the kids to be as prepared as possible but really could not predict with any specificity what they would find in terms of host families, housing, foods they would eat, activities in which they would participate, and so on. I could only assume that this group of young people from Ohio would most certainly want to swim in the Caribbean in mid-December.

The discipline of cross-cultural psychology and the applied field of intercultural or cross-cultural training are relatively recent endeavors that have evolved over the past thirty to forty years. Primarily used to assist businesspeople, diplomats, scholars, missionaries, and Peace Corps volunteers to better understand and successfully adapt to the experiences that occur when people from two or more cultures interact in some way, the field has much to offer both teachers and students.

Certain goals and objectives are common to all cross-cultural training programs. In general, cross-cultural training attempts to help people communicate more effectively, both in verbal and nonverbal modes; develop effective and meaningful interpersonal relationships; and reduce the stress that tends to accompany most intercultural experiences (Cushner and Brislin 1996). Cross-cultural training also seeks to help people reduce their ethnocentrism, guiding them to become more ethnorelative in their judgments about others. All these goals, incidentally, apply to domestic multicultural education programs as well as international or global education—all increasingly important as schools and communities become more diverse.

Attaining intercultural competence is a developmental process that evolves over a significant period of time as a result of a series of intense interpersonal interactions and opportunities. While traditional schooling may be good at imparting a significant amount of knowledge using such cognitive approaches as lectures, books, and film, there is a poor correlation between the attainment of knowledge and subsequent achievement of the goals of cross-cultural training, which, if looked at closely, are more behavioral and attitudinal in orientation. Culture learning thus requires a long-term, experiential approach to learning—the very thing that travel experience provides—coupled with the knowledge or cognitive inputs the classroom can offer. It is the blend of experience and knowledge that is critical.

The cross-cultural orientation of sojourners—temporary travelers entering a new society—can be approached from two possible vantage points. A culture-specific approach provides a significant amount of information that is unique to the target cultural group or destination. A culture-general approach focuses on the commonalities in the intercultural experience that all people are certain to encounter; such things as communication differences, confronting personal prejudice, and dealing with disconfirmed expectations. Good cross-cultural training programs integrate strategies and concepts from each because both have value. But in this particular circumstance, preparing children to travel to Belize, there were no culture-specific materials available to help prepare us for our experience. At the time, I really did not know much about the field of cross-cultural training anyway, as I only had my own travel experiences to draw upon. So I punted and, armed with the best of intentions, made it up as we went along. Little did I know that this would lead, in large measure, to a future direction in my career path.

Seventeen committed student travelers met for one hour every Monday after school to participate in a number of group-building activities and to prepare for what we *might* encounter. One advantage of having a school near a university was the possibility of coordinating field experiences for Spanish-language students interested in teaching basic Spanish. While no one expected the children to really learn the language to any degree of fluency in a few short months, they could at least develop some basic familiarity.

Preparation for the other eventualities, however, was another story. It is pretty certain in any travel experience that people will encounter all kinds of differences—they may just be difficult to predict. While in Mexico, our group would be staying in a small hotel in town; a "culture" with which most were familiar. While we were in Belize, however, accommodation would be with host families. Everyone wants these experiences to be as positive as possible and aims to avoid those embarrassing moments when a child, responding to someone's hospitality, screws up his or her face at some new food or unfamiliar behavior and lets out a groan of utter disgust.

Not knowing what food practices we would encounter on the trip, I would bring new and different-looking, but edible, food each Monday and provide it for the afternoon snack. This seemed to be a pretty good approach to "getting the yucks out" in the safety of the classroom before venturing into a new family situation where things would not be familiar, while encouraging the development of new eating habits. Each week the children would be presented with something they had never seen before—Middle Eastern dips that were unfamiliar, a variety of Mexican sauces that were not available in the local Taco Bell, that notorious Australian yeast extract Vegemite, and bottled gefilte fish usually eaten during the Jewish Passover holiday. This seemed to work fairly well; there were lots of "yucks" shared each Monday, and most went home hungry each time.

Chocolate-covered ants brought to class one Monday became the basis of a contest to see how many each student could eat. Only a few brave students would compete—most were not willing to even touch the stuff. John, a rather tall twelve-year-old who put on an air of machismo, was quite the show-off and proceeded to devour ant after ant, consuming at least twice as many as any other student. He won the competition but, to his embarrassment, quickly ran off and vomited in the restroom across the hall. He had to withstand weeks of ridicule after that.

During these sessions we also spent time discussing safe eating habits while on the road; such standard things as avoiding water or ice in beverages, not eating unpeeled raw fruits or vegetables, and not eating cream-based foods that may have been sitting, unrefrigerated, for some time. Perhaps I overdid some aspects, raising everyone's anxiety, but at the time I thought it better to be safe than sorry. And it was only many years later that I learned that a certain amount of anxiety is to be expected and is, in fact, beneficial to the cross-cultural experience.

It was also necessary to bring the parents together as our departure neared. A parents' evening was planned in the school in early December, about two weeks before we were to leave. I felt quite confident that all was in order. Three parent volunteers would join my wife, Hyla, and me as chaperones. With seventeen children between the ages of nine and twelve, the proportions seemed adequate.

Travel, as well as planning for travel, demands that one be flexible and able to accommodate most any circumstance that is confronted. And here was one of our first—weeks before we even got to the airport. Current events can have a major impact on people's perception of a particular place. Five days before our parent orientation meeting four nuns from northern Ohio were taken hostage and killed in El Salvador. I was certain, especially with all the publicity the story was receiving in the local papers, that most of the parents would pull their children from the experience. In preparation for the evening, one of the parents telephoned the U.S. Department of State for a travel advisory. He informed the group that the government was relatively unconcerned and that Belize was considered a safe place to travel because it was not too heavily engaged in the Central American political conflicts of the time. I guess those modern-day pirates I had read so much about in the travel guides really didn't amount to much.

We were off in just a few short weeks, busy now with last-minute planning meetings with the school principal and parents, making certain all our travel documents were in order, planning for a few days' stopover in Mexico, and deciding what kinds of gifts and cultural artifacts we would bring along. All went well in this regard as we patiently waited for our departure day to arrive.

❸

TRAVELING WITH CLASS: THE TRIP BEGINS

Be prepared; then let go of expectations.

—P. Cosineau

Cross-cultural orientation, in general, is designed to reduce the intensity of the inevitable culture shock that accompanies travel to foreign destinations. While people generally expect to encounter differences in such areas as language, food, and the manner in which things are done, they are often surprised at how quickly and how strongly their emotions are engaged.

The real test of the effectiveness of cross-cultural orientation begins almost immediately after departure—especially with children. Tears flowed among our travelers to Mexico as children and parents said their good-byes to one another, each knowing that this would be their first Christmas away from one another. Unfortunately, I hadn't given this as much forethought as I should have. Here I was, a Jewish teacher in a non-Jewish community, focused on cross-cultural and international activities, giving scant attention to the meaning of the holiday in the lives of these children. Oh, what I was to learn!

The plane ride was uneventful, thankfully, as most are. This group of young travelers felt quite comfortable, and mature, as they moved freely among all the passengers on the plane, proudly telling others of the adventure that was forthcoming. They were the center of much attention from the flight attendants and passengers throughout the entire trip as connections were made in Miami for a final destination in Mérida.

I was not prepared for our arrival, with seventeen children and five adults, into the crowded, noisy Mérida airport filled with people coming and going as the holiday season approached. My wife, Hyla, almost instinctively knowing what to do, stepped into action, grouping children, parents, and baggage once we cleared customs while I went about searching for the transportation we had arranged to take us to the hotel.

"Excuse me," someone said as he tapped me on the shoulder.

"I don't need your help," I blurted out, anticipating that onslaught of taxi drivers and other locals who would, like vultures circling overhead waiting for an animal to finally give in and die, see me as the vulnerable newcomer that I was. I wasn't about to relent so early in the experience; we hadn't even left the airport.

"Are you Ken Cushner?" the voice asked.

OK, now he had my attention.

The soft-spoken man continued, in perfect English, "My name is Enrique and I am the head of the English Department at Colegio Peninsular, Rogers Hall School. The American consulate sent me your letter a few weeks ago. I'd like you and your students to come to our school tomorrow, spend the last morning before the holiday break with us, and then we'll take you to some of the Mayan ruins in the region. If it's OK with you, we'll pick you up at your hotel at 9:00 A.M."

If it's OK with me, I thought?

"What a pleasant surprise," I responded, not quite convinced that he was for real.

Who could have wished for anything more? A chance to spend a day in a school and share in some social time with local Mexican students! This was a dream come true. I shared this information with the group once we were on the bus and on our way to the hotel.

As we checked into our city hotel I told the children to meet me in the café in about an hour for a light meal. This would give everyone a chance to unpack and explore his or her new surroundings, and it would give Hyla and me some time to unwind.

The kids were talkative and energetic as they came running down the stairwell toward the lobby and into the café. I gathered them at a few tables in a far corner along a wall. There was a wine cart in the corner. Among the bottles of wine on the cart was a can of Raid insecticide. That didn't bother me. What startled me, though, was a sign on the cart that said, "The manager has personally passed all the water used in the hotel." Now wasn't that comforting. I knew then that we were in for more than a few surprises.

Hyla and I listened in on some of the conversations of the students as they settled into their chairs.

"Do you believe it's all in Spanish?" laughed Julie. "I tried to turn on the air conditioner and the dials were all in Spanish. How am I supposed to make it work?"

Confronting disconfirmed expectations is quite common for travelers, especially in the early phases of an experience, when one's emotions are highly engaged (Cushner and Brislin 1996). In this case, both the student and I saw our expectations disconfirmed. During preparation for travel, people tend to construe certain images and expectations of what the new setting will be like as well as how they will respond in this new situation. And these expectations are generally positive and exciting. The reality of what is encountered, however, is oftentimes inconsistent with the image conjured up in the mind. The ability to reconcile this difference is one key to a smooth transition in the early stages of an intercultural experience. It was suddenly apparent to me that all the orientation and language training we had undergone may not have done the job that I had assumed it had. Julie acted as if the fact that everything was in Spanish came as a complete surprise. This really disturbed me, as we had spent four months studying Spanish during our weekly orientation sessions. For Julie there seemed to be no connection between what we had done in the classroom and the reality that she now faced.

Researchers in the field of cross-cultural training have discovered a few unanticipated and noncommonsense surprises in the intercultural experience, and this was one of them. That is, cross-cultural orientation, at least at the outset, may not be as meaningful to participants who have not had direct and personal intercultural experiences they can draw upon. This is supported by learning theorists and cognitive psychologists who suggest that a significant portion of what people learn in any learning situation, in some cases up to 70 percent, is directly dependent upon what the individual already knows. One of the major tasks of any good educator or trainer, then, is to stimulate the student's prior knowledge so new information is added to this foundation. If people do not have prior knowledge—or, in this case, cross-cultural experience—new concepts may "come in one ear and go out the other," so to speak. Those who have had few, if any, significant intercultural experiences are thus at a disadvantage when it comes to cross-cultural orientation. Julie was demonstrating this reality.

Research goes on to suggest that cross-cultural training may be most effective once people have embarked on their sojourn and have some direct experience they can fall back upon. Therein lies the dilemma. How do people who have had little intercultural experience best prepare for the eventualities they are certain to encounter? This is one of the tasks that face all who work to prepare people for cross-cultural encounters. Perhaps it would be now, after the children had begun having some direct experiences, that cross-cultural training would be most meaningful. But in this particular situation there was little time in the schedule to accommodate classroom-oriented instruction. These issues would have to be addressed as best they could be as the days unfolded—on buses, in waiting lounges, over common meals, and so forth.

Once the meals were ordered, Hyla and I moved between the tables to make sure everything was in order. Susan, who had skipped a grade early in her schooling, was the youngest of the children traveling with us, at nine years old. I thought that pretty impressive—that a child as young as Susan would venture away with us for so long. And what was perhaps even more impressive was that her mother had no hesitation about sending her with us. Susan was in tears, though, when I approached her table after the meals arrived.

"I can't eat this stuff," she cried. "You told us not to eat mayonnaise. And look at this. My sandwich has mayonnaise all over it."

"No problem," I said. "Just send it back and tell the waiter you don't want anything on your sandwich."

Sounded simple enough. I helped Susan communicate this, or so I thought, as we spoke slowly to the waiter in English and very broken Spanish. Five minutes later, I looked back and Susan was in tears again.

"All he did was change the bread," she cried. "The mayonnaise is still all over the meat! And what is this stuff?" she yelled, pointing to a side dish of what I assumed to be refried beans that had been placed in front of everyone. "It looks like I got sick right here on the plate. How disgusting!" I had to agree with her; it did look more like a cow pie than any refried beans I had ever seen at my local Mexican restaurant.

"I can't eat this, Mr. C. I want to go home." And she continued to cry.

One day into this trip and I was confronting the beginnings of culture shock and homesickness in these young students. Rather early in the trip, I thought, but nevertheless real and something to contend with.

As long ago as 1960, the anthropologist Kalvero Oberg coined the term "culture-shock" to refer to the anxiety and stress that results when a person living or working in an overseas context loses many of the familiar signs and symbols to which he or she has become accustomed, while going about trying to satisfy his or her everyday needs. It is a rather generalized description of the responses people experience when things do not go as expected in a new cultural setting, when there is a general inability to make sense of the new stimuli to which one is exposed, or when one's own behavior does not produce the expected results.

Culture shock is not a disease or something that only unsuccessful people experience, as is often thought. It is a perfectly normal response and an ongoing process that seems essential to learning in the new setting. Culture shock is a rather broad construct that is experienced when people encounter differences in such areas as verbal and nonverbal communication; the varying orientations people have toward time and space; and the more subtle and intangible aspects of people, such as their differences in attitudes, behavioral norms, and the underlying values people defend as fundamental to their lives. Other differences, too, such as those in the physical places one encounters while traveling; in the technologies used; in the power, social structure, and support that people have; and in what is seen, heard, felt, and even smelled and tasted, can also affect the traveler. Such is the essence of what may contribute to culture shock.

How one accommodates these experiences, though, is critical. If people react negatively, common responses such as alienation, anxiety, resentment, a high degree of stress, and anger—none of which facilitate adjustment—may result. If travelers can anticipate some of the differences they are likely to encounter ahead of time, and can develop healthy strategies to respond to such changes, they are less likely to be debilitated when they encounter these differences. Helping people accomplish this is the role and function of good orientation and training programs.

Culture-specific training is successful when one is preparing people for interactions that will be restricted to one culture or when a significant amount of information is known about a particular group. In most instances, particularly in contexts that are as culturally diverse as American schools and communities, people encounter a wide variety of cultures. Even in settings that appear to be rather homogeneous in makeup, people encounter a wide diversity of cultures in their professional and adult life. And an expanded definition of culture includes aspects related to social class, gender, ability, sexual orientation, and so on. Culture-general training thus has much to offer educators.

Over the years, a number of cross-cultural training strategies have been developed, many of which have proved to have varying degrees of positive impact. Among the most extensively researched and useful cross-cultural training strategies in educational settings is the culture assimilator or intercultural sensitizer (Cushner and Landis 1996). In this approach, trainees or students read a number of critical incidents, or short stories, that depict individuals from two or more cultures who encounter some problem due to miscommunication or misunderstanding. The reader is then asked to select from three or four alternative choices the one that best explains the problem from the other culture's perspective.

Intercultural sensitizers were initially developed for culture-specific situations; to prepare Australian bankers to live and work in Thailand, or American adolescents to work with Honduran villagers in Amigos de las Americas volunteer programs, for instance. While culture-specific sensitizers are extremely beneficial, their use is rather restricted because of their cultural specificity and lack of widespread availability due to their development for relatively small and role-specific groups.

A culture-general sensitizer or assimilator was later developed to prepare people for the kinds of experiences they are certain to encounter in their intercultural interactions (Brislin et al. 1986; Cushner and Brislin 1996). Similar in structure to the culture-specific forerunner, this tool uses the critical-incident format to introduce people to eighteen

TRAVELING WITH CLASS: THE TRIP BEGINS 33

culture-general themes that they are certain to encounter regardless of their background or with whom they will interact. These eighteen themes fall into three general categories. The Knowledge Areas category introduces readers to eight themes that all cultures define and learn, albeit differently, including work orientation, time and spatial orientation, roles, communication, group versus individual orientation, rituals and superstitions, class and status, and values. The Bases of Cultural Differences category encompasses five themes that address the manner in which people process information and includes categorization, differentiation, in-group and out-group distinction, learning-style differences, and attribution formation. Finally, five themes fall under Experiences that Engage the Emotions, including anxiety, the need to belong, ambiguity, confrontation with prejudice in self and others, and disconfirmed expectations—all of which seemed at play early in the experience with my young travelers.

Early the next morning, Hyla and I went from room to room knocking on doors, reminding the children to meet in the lobby at seven o'clock so we could have breakfast before our bus arrived. Venturing down the street, we found a suitable restaurant. Susan was a bit more relaxed as she sat with Hyla and me and ate her first breakfast of huevos rancheros, a tortilla topped with fried egg and a mild sauce. I noticed she left the beans untouched on the side of her plate, as did most of the children. At least there were no more "yucks" coming from the group.

Not wanting to miss our 9:00 A.M. bus, I rushed the kids back from the restaurant to the hotel. The kids ran up and down the stairs between the lobby and their rooms while I paced back and forth in the lobby, looking for our bus. Fifteen minutes passed, with no bus and no Enrique. Thirty minutes later and still no bus. Now I was really getting worried, and I continued to pace, going in and out the door from the lobby to the street, hoping to catch a glimpse of a bus. The kids were getting worse and were almost impossible to control. Running through the lobby, in and out of the café, and up and down the stairs, they went just about anywhere their little legs would take them. Oh, what would they be like in the school, I wondered, *if* we ever got there? Forty-five minutes and still no Enrique. I had no idea what to do. I couldn't call the school as I hardly recalled the name of it. So I continued to pace and worry.

Finally, after more than an hour, a bus weaved its way down our winding street and pulled up in front of the hotel. Enrique climbed down, greeted me with "hola," as if we'd been long lost friends, and mumbled something quickly about being a bit late. A *bit* late, I thought. This was more than an hour after he'd said he'd pick us up.

"Remember, this is Mexico," he said, as I confided that I had been getting a bit worried. "Time takes on a new meaning here, and you'd better get used to it."

My American, or better yet, my United States culture, was operating in full force, as I, like my young students, fell victim to my own cultural conditioning. This would not be the first instance where a difference in time orientation would cause me to feel those strong emotions associated with anxiety and ambiguity.

Our day at the school was far more than we could have hoped for. This was the last day of school before the holiday break, and we spent the morning attending a variety of classes and joining in on holiday celebrations. Most fun for all was the breaking of piñatas. And our kids got quite involved. Blindfolded and swinging away, they seemed like naturals, while displaying an openness and willingness of spirit that endeared them to all in the school. I was quite pleased and proud of our group of young travelers.

Enrique invited a number of his students to join us for lunch, followed by an outing to Uxmal, one of the largest of the ancient cities of the Yucatán Peninsula. Located about an hour south of Mérida, Uxmal was home to about 25,000 Maya, flourishing between 600 and 900 C.E. Carvings most commonly found at the site include serpents and latticework, along with masks of the god Chac, the god of rain, who was greatly revered by the Maya because of the lack of natural water supplies in the city. It was to Chac, Enrique would tell the group, that human sacrifices were performed at the highest temple of the site—the House of the Magician. With the victim still alive, the priest would rip out the heart of the sacrificed soul with a flint knife and throw the body, allegedly still moving, down the steep steps. It was thought to be an honor to have been chosen for this rite. My students were fully engrossed in Enrique's storytelling, and perhaps grossed out by such detail and gruesomeness of the stories. But it was certainly a motivator to encourage them to want to learn more.

Our adventure in Mexico far exceeded my expectations. And I truly enjoyed getting to know Enrique. This relationship alone developed into an exchange between our two schools that lasted for three years. Each year I would take as many as forty students to Mérida and Enrique would bring an equal number of his students to Ohio. And in more recent years, Enrique has begun hosting my student teachers in local schools in and around Mérida. But for now, it's on to Belize—and other cultural surprises.

4

THE POWER OF TRAVEL OCCURS OFF THE BEATEN TRACK

Keeping to the main road is easy, but people love to be sidetracked.

—Lao-tzu, sixth century B.C.E.

The kids were understandably quite bored and tired from traveling by bus for six hours by the time we reached Belize City, and they were begging for some free time to explore and move their legs. But given all I'd read about Belize City—this bastion of crime, criminals, and drugs—I was not about to let them out of my sight to go traipsing around a strange city, even if they did feel confident and sure. We were able to busy ourselves in and around the bus station where we stopped for a break. I couldn't figure out what was happening at first, but the kids kept running in and out of the restrooms the whole time we were there. It wasn't until I went into the men's room to investigate that it all became comically clear.

Another difference to get used to—toilets! The kids discovered that an open sewage system was in use and created their own game. One by one, each child would sit on the toilet, release yesterday's lunch, and flush it down the toilet, and then they would all run outside to see if they could beat their business before it dropped into the open sewer that ran alongside the station. And this was in the capital city! I really began to worry about what we'd find once we arrived in a small village.

We had arrived a day earlier in Chetumal, a rather drab and boring town on the border between Mexico and Belize, without much of a problem, having traveled from Mérida for six hours by public bus. I was relieved when the bus driver who would take us into Belize found us at the agreed-upon hotel. And what a surprise it was to find that our bus was nothing more than an old, retired, yellow American school bus that had found its way to Belize to serve as major transportation throughout the country. What a sight we must have been: twenty-two of us rolling along through the countryside as if we were on a field trip from school. It was a field trip of sorts, but not like one most children, or teachers for that matter, would ever take back home.

We left Chetumal early in the morning for our long journey south, which would take us through most of Belize. The driver could only guess at how long it might take to reach Dangriga, our destination, some 120 miles away, estimating anywhere from ten to fourteen hours. One hundred and twenty miles in ten hours—and that was the quickest route! What could he be thinking?

Driving time in Belize, our driver informed us, depended on a number of factors, including how often and for how long we needed to stop, the conditions of the road along the way, and a bit of luck that we would make the trip without breaking down. As we would soon find out, our driver was correct, and we had all those things to worry about. The roads in Belize, for one, leave much to be desired. We would dodge pothole after pothole on a road that looked to be not much different from the surface of the moon, as we zigzagged our way along at a top speed of twenty miles per hour. But we could never maintain that speed for long.

Our route took us south through the towns of Corozal, Pembroke Hall, and Orange Walk (where we stopped for a lunch that consisted of grilled cheese sandwiches and fries for twenty-two but never did see anything that resembled an orange walk anywhere), and then into Belize City. From this former capital, we continued on to the new capital, Belmopan, built inland not too many years before, when people grew tired of cleaning up after hurricanes. We continued south, traveling through rainforests and citrus groves, and eventually worked our way to Dangriga, the roads getting increasingly rough and narrow the farther south we drove. At one point we approached a one-lane bridge so narrow that the driver, fearing we might get wedged along the road and then be unable to exit using the door, had us all get off the bus while he maneuvered, inch by inch, to the other side. Mark, one of the parents traveling along with us, was a psychologist who worked with people's phobias. He ran off the bus with camera in hand, photographing the entire ordeal, planning to use the photos as a means to help some of his patients overcome their fear of small spaces.

We arrived in the village just before sunset. About one hundred people followed along as the bus pulled into town, with Nikita, Leroy, Louise, and Anna leading the crowd. General introductions were made; children were matched with host families; and all went to their respective homes for their first encounter with their new friends. The adults were taken to the one hotel in town, which would serve as a base. We had the only available phone, and the children knew where they could find us if they needed anything. We would have a formal program of introductions and presentation in the morning.

Numerous companies exist that provide group travel experiences for school students, offering teachers free travel for every six to ten participants they can enlist. Such organizations can make it easy for teachers and students to travel to many countries in the world for sightseeing. There is a downside of such trips, however. Groups of teachers and students, encapsulated in buses and tourist-class hotels, visit monuments, museums, and mansions at the expense of having meaningful, in-depth contact with host nationals. Any cross-cultural experience that is encountered tends to be at a surface or tourist level; this level of culture is often referred to as *objective culture*. International or intercultural experiences that impact the more profound levels of culture learning, however, do not simply happen—they evolve slowly over time and as a result of long-term engagement. Understanding this deeper level of culture is referred to as *subjective culture*.

There is a critical distinction between objective and subjective levels of culture that is essential for the educator to understand (Triandis 1972). Objective culture refers to the visible or tangible elements of a culture: such aspects as the artifacts made, the clothing worn, the foods eaten, and sometimes the names given to things. Objective cultural elements are easy to see and touch, and people generally agree upon what it is that they can observe. Such elements, however, are not the aspects of culture that are most critical and meaningful; nor are they the ones that lead to the problems people generally encounter in communication or interpersonal or group conflict.

The more profound and meaningful levels of culture operate at the subjective level, existing beneath the surface. Subjective culture refers to the intangible, invisible aspects of a people—such as the attitudes people bring with them to any interaction, the expectations they have of others, and the values they may hold about such things as education, elders, or another group of people. Many of the concepts introduced in the eighteen-theme culture-general framework provide examples of subjective culture (Cushner and Brislin 1996). These aspects of culture are much more difficult to put on a table to see and discuss, yet they are at play in all interactions.

In addressing subjective elements of culture, people learn about such things as others' historical experiences, their previous interactions with other groups, and the expectations they may have of others. They begin to understand why people do the things that they do, why they communicate in the manner in which they do, and why they behave in ways that may appear, at the outset, to be quite different and perhaps confrontational. Such an understanding and orientation allows people to get beyond the initial and oftentimes negative reactions to meeting someone new and different, thus encouraging continuation of a relationship.

The iceberg is often used as an analogy to explain the distinction between objective and subjective culture. Typically, about 10 percent of an iceberg's mass appears above the surface of the water; this portion of the iceberg can be likened to objective culture. Objective culture is the tangible and visible elements of people that are easy for all to see.

Ninety percent of the iceberg, however, lies beneath the surface of the water, invisible to the naked eye. This is the portion that is of most concern to the ship's captain and can do the most damage to the ship. So it is with subjective culture. Understanding these deeper elements, such as the assumptions people make and the attitudes they hold, are fundamental to the success of any intercultural interaction, yet they are not readily visible to the casual observer. Good intercultural education and culture learning must focus on the subjective level of culture. It is through influential and meaningful travel experiences that subjective levels of culture can be reached.

The children really had no idea what they were in for when they agreed to go on this venture. They were coming from a comfortable middle-class community where they had most of the comforts and privileges anyone would have wanted—private bedrooms, fully equipped kitchens, well-stocked refrigerators, and the like. Here in Dangriga, they had the opportunity to experience, firsthand, many of the things that they could only read about in their textbooks back home. Our hosts opened up their lives and homes, providing their guests with all the comforts that they could. Even though most families had relatively little, they were more than willing to share all of it; such is the nature of Belizean hospitality. Most of the homes, for instance, consisted of no more than two or three rooms, and, in many cases, two or three children shared a bed. Our hosts vacated these beds so our kids could have a bit of the comfort they assumed they would need.

Children in many of the families were given the opportunity to assist with meal preparation. Many of them, for instance, had the chance to point out which chicken from under the house they wanted for dinner and then help with its preparation. Or, going to the river, children could help in the hunt for "bamboo chickens"—iguanas that grow much larger than the typical pet-store variety and are considered a local delicacy. The kids certainly had plenty of opportunity to experience things they would rarely have the chance to do elsewhere. I'm not sure how many became vegetarians during their stay, but I'm sure the trip prompted some serious contemplation of the matter.

One of our students, John, the macho young man who had eaten all those chocolate-covered ants during orientation, was staying with a family not too far from the hotel. Late in the afternoon of the second day, after our morning welcome session at the community center and after the kids had gone back for time with their families, his host mother came to us, worried because he had been complaining of stomachaches. Here we go, I thought; we were already having to deal with problems caused by food, and we'd only been in town for one full day. Hyla and I went to see John. Sure enough, he was doubled up in pain, complaining about his stomach and asking if he could come spend the night with us. The family gave us some private time with him. After a while John relaxed. His real problem, it seemed, was not food related at all but a psychologically oriented adjustment problem. This macho young man of twelve years old had been placed in a family of five young girls. Aside from the father, there were no other males in the family, and he was just uncomfortable with the entire situation. Once this was established and communicated we were able to make the necessary change of families—and all were happier as a result. Subjective cultural differences of another kind were certainly at work here.

Even though it was school holidays, our days were filled with immeasurable educational activities. We would meet each morning at the community center for a joint activity that differed each day. On the first full day we participated in a welcoming ceremony attended by many of the village elders, the mayor, all the school officials, and many children and their families. It was quite a moving experience presenting a world atlas signed by all the children in our school, including those who could not travel with us. This gift, it turned out, represented the first book owned by the school—something that my students just could not understand. On another day we presented brief plays about life in Ohio to the children. It was awkward, to say the least, to dramatize snow onstage to an audience who, for the most part, had never actually seen or felt the stuff—and all this in seventy-degree weather with a backdrop of the Caribbean!

Each of these miniadventures presented opportunities for all to grow. One day we ventured out to one of the nearby cays to eat lunch and to snorkel along the Northern Hemisphere's largest barrier reef, which is second in size only to the Great Barrier Reef in Australia. What an exhilarating day we all had as we stopped for lunch and walked along the shoreline of a nearby uninhabited island among the coral and colorful fish.

At one point, Karen, an adventurous young girl of eleven, had strolled quite a distance from shore. We weren't sure what could have been wrong, but Karen began yelling to us to come and save her—yet she was only standing in ankle-deep water. Hyla went out to her as quickly as she could, stepping as carefully as possible to avoid damaging the coral. When she reached her, Karen grabbed onto Hyla's arm as tightly as she could. There was no apparent danger—Karen, it seemed, had simply panicked. Focusing at her feet and walking amid a new environment consisting of fish, coral, sea urchins, and other marine life, she simply became overly anxious about her surroundings as well as her ability to manipulate through the maze of activity.

Christmas in Belize, the children soon realized, was celebrated quite differently than back home. The American children were accustomed to lavish holiday displays and huge trees adorning each and every home. In Belize, the celebration was much more subdued; and the children did not anticipate this. Trees, if they were displayed in the homes at all, were never more than two or three feet tall; they looked more like small bushes than the trees to which the children were accustomed. And there were few, if any, presents lying beneath waiting to be opened—and none, it seemed, for those over twelve years of age. What a disappointment for my students.

And with that realization, the tears began to flow—for two days. Sometimes it's difficult to differentiate culture shock from homesickness, and in this case, it didn't matter. One just led to the other. For the next two days all we had were miserable children, moping around, dreaming of sugarplum fairies and whatever other holiday memories were on their minds. This didn't happen all at once, mind you. Children's moodiness seemed to ebb and flow. But once one or two became upset, it caught on like wildfire and we had to deal with everyone all at once. It eventually became nonstop tears, and a losing battle.

We finally hatched a plan. The children were staying in homes that had no telephones. Since Hyla and I had the only telephone available in our hotel, we would allow the children each to make a five-minute call home from our room, basically as a way to reassure them that their Christmas presents would be waiting for them upon their return. Some even had to beg their parents to keep the Christmas tree until they returned home. This seemed to do the trick. The children were all reminded that they were still loved; that they were missed; and that they would celebrate upon their return. And Hyla and I vowed that the only children we would take on a trip at Christmastime again were Jewish children to Israel or others to the North Pole.

While traditional educational efforts tend to be rather slow at bringing about the needed shift in one's thinking, travel affords one the opportunity, and often forces one, to see and confront the world from another perspective. We all left this experience renewed and refreshed, having learned an untold amount, much of which would not even be known until long after our return. We also left committed to maintaining our relationship with the community.

The experience of giving the school its first book, for instance, made an enormous impression on the children, none of whom could fathom that a school could exist without books. Even before we left Dangriga, the students had decided to do something to change the situation that they had encountered. When they returned home, the students started an after-school snack bar that raised enough money to ship more than 500 donated books to the school! This is exactly the kind of social-action response a teacher would hope to see—people becoming involved in ways and in activities where they felt they could make a difference. And this was the result of a firsthand travel encounter, thus reinforcing the important role of lived experience in the attainment of a global perspective and commitment. But more on the impact of travel later in the book.

5

LEARNING TO TRAVEL IS LEARNING TO SEE: DEVELOPING INTERCULTURAL SENSITIVITY

> The real voyage of discovery consists not in seeing new landscapes, but in having new eyes.
>
> —Marcel Proust

The lessons learned while traveling can be unanticipated and quite profound and can have an unexpected impact. Travel affords one the opportunity to see the world from another perspective. But these lessons don't always jump right out at you. More often than not, they are missed because of one's inability to perceive what has gone on from the local perspective, or one's inability to step back from the situation. Good teachers make it a priority to take the time to help their students reflect upon what they are encountering and discuss what they have learned. When one does not have others to help guide reflection, it may take time for the lesson to become evident.

My wife and I had been planning our own trip through Kenya as preparation for taking a group of teachers on safari following an international conference the next year. We had done our homework before leaving and knew the areas of the country that we wanted to visit. We did not want to be too prescriptive or packaged with our plans; instead we would allow many of the day-to-day details to unfold once we began our travels. After spending an initial week in Nairobi familiarizing ourselves with the people and collecting the necessary gear, we would rent a jeep and make our way between the Masai Mara, Samburu, and Amboseli game reserves.

Prior to leaving Nairobi we were warned about travel through Nakuru, Kenya's fourth largest town, located halfway between Nairobi and Kisumu on Lake Victoria. Travelers, it seemed, were the object of numerous scams whereby unsuspecting drivers passing through town would be motioned by numerous people pointing to the front of their car. After pulling over and being told there was something wrong—smoke was visible or the car was shaking—they would be directed to a local garage, which just happened to be operated by a friend of their new "savior." The garage would, of course, repair the car, the bill totaling many hundreds of dollars, for what would end up being unnecessary repairs. Oh, for the blessings of a new friend.

But we were ready. This would never happen to us. We were aware and would have our guard up. Trusting as we were, we wouldn't be taken by any novice criminals.

We were driving south on our way to Amboseli and Mount Kilimanjaro after three glorious days of photographing wildlife in the desertlike environs of Samburu National Park when we came upon Nakuru, after being on the road for about six hours. A bit hungry, but not wanting to stay long, we decided to stop at the Kenya Coffee House on the corner of Moi Road and Kenyatta Avenue. Our guidebook suggested that this was the best place in town to get a good cup of coffee.

After considerable negotiation of the local streets we found the Kenya Coffee House near the center of town. We felt lucky not to have confronted any auto hustlers along the way, and we parked along Moi Road, just around the corner from the coffee shop. In front of us were a number of small shops—a pharmacy, a seamstress, a fruit stall—and what seemed like hundreds of people milling about.

"I don't feel right about this place," Hyla cautioned, grabbing my hand as we got out of the vehicle. "I don't think we should stay here."

"Oh, don't be silly," I replied. "We're only going to stop for ten minutes to get a cup of coffee. Let's lock the jeep. Now, walk with intention, letting others think we know where we're going." The phrase "walk with intention" had become a mantra I found myself repeating quite often on

LEARNING TO TRAVEL IS LEARNING TO SEE

this trip, hoping that if it looked as if we knew where we were going we would have fewer encounters with shady characters.

"I don't know," Hyla said. "I just don't feel right." I grabbed my backpack, which held our passports, tickets, and camera, locked the vehicle, and off we went.

It was hardly ten minutes later when we left the shop, feeling somewhat disappointed—I couldn't believe that was the best coffee Kenya had to offer. Upon rounding the corner, I noticed that the doors of our jeep were wide open. My stomach knotted as I grabbed Hyla's arm and told her I thought we had been robbed. We raced back to the jeep. Sure enough, every door was wide open, and all our luggage was missing. We frantically checked all over, hoping that somehow we'd overlooked something. But no luck. Everything was gone. We began asking those standing in the doorways of the shops and on the walkway if they'd seen anything. Not a word! A hundred people stood around and watched as our vehicle was cleaned out and no one saw a thing! How baffling.

We were angry, to say the least. Not knowing what to do, we began driving around town, hoping that perhaps we might see our bags being shuffled off by someone. No luck. We wanted, no, *needed*, our luggage. I, at least, had left a suitcase back in a hotel, and we could continue on our trip, going back through Nairobi to pick it up. Hyla, however, had all of her belongings in the jeep, and they were nowhere to be found. I could hear it all now. "I told you so! I didn't feel right about this place! Walk with intention?" Thankfully, none of that was forthcoming.

We drove to the market, thinking that perhaps we'd see our things already on display and being sold in some used clothing stall. Again, no luck. What we really did not want to lose were the twelve rolls of exposed film that documented our adventures and the notebook that contained the names and addresses of people we had met along the way who would help to put our group together the following year. Before leaving town we wrote a brief classified ad and left it with the local newspaper asking—no, pleading—for the return of our film and notebooks. And we filed a report with the local police.

We were furious and felt violated when we left Nakuru, angry with ourselves for trusting enough to leave our belongings unattended. But that was our nature. We had been in Kenya for almost two weeks and had developed a certain level of trust and comfort. With all the warnings about theft and muggings in Nairobi, or "Nairobbery," as it is sometimes called, and especially the warnings about Nakuru, we should have been more careful. And I should have listened to my wife's gut feelings.

In between bursts of anger we left town, without a plan. Wouldn't you know it—just when we got to the outskirts of town, young men and boys started pointing frantically at the front of our jeep. No way were we going to succumb to that game. This helped turn our anger to laughter as we drove as fast as we could from town. We did, however, stop to check the front of our vehicle every now and then, just as a measure of safety.

What to do? We couldn't continue as planned, as neither of us had anything to wear. We decided to return to Nairobi, pick up my remaining suitcase, and see about getting some new clothes. We called ahead to our lodge in Amboseli and postponed our arrival by one day. We also called the hotel we had used earlier in Nairobi to see about staying the night. No problem. Both places were understanding and quite accommodating. At least we had found the caring human spirit once again.

Our shopping spree was like nothing we had ever done before. We were not certain of what we should buy. Most of the clothes were not of a style we would wear at home. The pants, underwear, and even the socks seemed to fit differently. We decided on a few T-shirts—at least we'd have some souvenirs when we returned home. We also grabbed a few pairs of pants and shorts, running shoes for my wife, and other things we thought we'd need for the remainder of our trip. Our Visa and American Express cards came in quite handy. A nice dinner at the hotel helped us make the transition to the return to the road.

The remainder of the trip was pleasant and, thankfully, uneventful. We never did see those photos or retrieve the names of the people we had met along the way. We did learn some valuable lessons that became evident not long after we returned home. There are some incredible inequities on the planet, and they had just been pointed out to us, and we found it difficult to continue to hold onto our anger much longer.

We had been violated—no doubt about that. But we had not been physically threatened. We had traveled through a country where the majority of the people live at or below the poverty level, many subsisting from day to day on whatever they are able to gather from their immediate environment. Perhaps it is a carryover from our hunting and gathering days, where whatever was available in the surroundings and not rooted to the ground or bigger or stronger than you became fair game. Our luggage certainly fit that category. So be it. We represented wealth beyond most people's imagination, carrying in our suitcases more clothes and belongings than many would have in their lifetime. Those who took our belongings did so without putting us in harm's way. During our entire trip we never felt threatened. Most people were gracious, if not interested and inquisitive, as were we.

And it was embarrassingly easy for us to replace our lost items. Thanks to plastic in our pockets, we were given endless credit to purchase whatever it was we wanted. And to top it off, upon our return home we were able to recoup 90 percent of our loss on our homeowner's insurance policy.

When questioning what is fair and what is equitable in a global society, one must ask, "Who are the criminals? What is to blame for these incredible global imbalances? How does a lifestyle and behavior in the developed world contribute to the poverty and behavior of others in a developing country like Kenya—even the auto scam artists?"

These are questions and issues that most people never confront. Yet these may be the very questions that lie at the base of much of the social unrest and discontent experienced by people across the planet. In some small way, perhaps we contributed to the welfare of a few who, now having our belongings, might otherwise have very little. And in one major way, this engaging experience taught us much more than any classroom lesson could ever accomplish. A small price to pay for an important lesson. Can we help our students grow from similar experiences?

Both cross-cultural orientation and intercultural education have interrelated and multifaceted goals, and both can have long-term as well as short-term objectives and outcomes. That is, in the short term, orientation experiences can facilitate an individual's transition for an immediate and upcoming sojourn. In the long run, the concepts introduced through orientation and developed and examined throughout an intercultural experience can significantly alter the way one understands, interprets, and interacts with others in the world.

An archaeologist sifts through layer upon layer of soil in an attempt to better understand the patterns that reflect the progression, development, and impact that have occurred at a given site over time. In a similar manner, interculturally skilled teachers look for patterns that emerge in their students' behavior, thoughts, perceptions, and dreams as they learn to reinterpret and then redefine their understanding of another's reality. Opening up the means of perception so people are able to see and interpret things differently than they did prior to an intercultural experience becomes one of the long-term goals of orientation and a subsequent intercultural experience. With this new understanding, people are then able to progress from a rather narrow, self-absorbed, and ethnocentric orientation to one that is more ethnorelative, open, inclusive, empathic, and interculturally sensitive and aware.

But predeparture orientation really only begins to scratch the surface of what is necessary to become interculturally skilled. Individuals must ultimately embark upon a sojourn that fully engages their cognitive, affective, and behavioral domains. It is the kinds of experiences that students have while in country that become critical to achieving the desired goals of meaningful international travel. And the teacher is the significant force in the design of this plan.

Everything people perceive in their environment is filtered through a certain set of lenses that operate to bring meaning to the stimuli in their world. Ethnocentrism refers to the tendency people have to interpret the world and judge others according to their own culture's lens, or standards. While a certain degree of ethnocentrism is essential in that it serves to bind a group of people together, it can become a serious obstacle when those who have internalized different ideas and behaviors begin to interact with one another. A statement Thomas Jefferson made in the mid-1800s comparing "sophisticated and cultured" Europeans to the native people of the Americas demonstrates how such an orientation and perspective enters our collective mind-set and then is applied across entire groups of people. Jefferson wrote (cited in Pearce 1965):

> Let a philosophic observer commence a journey from the *savages* of the Rocky Mountains, eastwardly towards the seacoast. These he would observe in the earliest stages of association, living under no law but that of nature, subsisting and covering themselves with the flesh and skins of wild beasts. He would next find those on the frontiers in the *pastoral stage*,

raising domestic animals to supply the advances of *civilization*, and so on in his progress he would meet the gradual shades of *improving man* until he would reach his, as yet, most improved state in our seaport towns. This, in fact, is equivalent to a survey, in time, of the progress of man from the infancy of creation to the present day. (155)

Such a statement helps us to understand how hierarchical terminology, such as First World versus Third World, or developed nation versus underdeveloped nation, easily finds its way into people's thinking and vocabulary. It is then perpetuated throughout a society and becomes quite difficult to reduce or eliminate.

One of the major consequences of ethnocentrism is the tendency people have to resist change. If people believe that their way of doing things is best, and if they have the power to choose to continue in familiar ways, why should they change? Consider the case of the United States and the adoption of the metric system. At this time, *all* other countries of the world have adopted the metric system as their primary means of measurement. The United States is the only country to hold on to something it feels is very dear to it, despite the difficulties this causes travelers, manufacturers, scientists, and others who must interact in a variety of ways with people from other nations. The failure of NASA scientists to convert English measures to metric values was the cause of the September 1999 loss of the Orbiter, a spacecraft that smashed into the planet Mars instead of reaching a safe orbit. This slight oversight resulted in the destruction of a $125 million spacecraft and jeopardized the entire Mars program until the successful landing of Spirit in 2004.

Intercultural educators strive to help people reduce their tendency to respond from an ethnocentric perspective and grow in terms of their understanding of, as well as their openness and skill in interacting with, those who are different. This is no simple task given what we know about how people learn about culture and the inherent obstacles and resistance to change most people exhibit. We are thus left with many questions: Just what does it mean to be interculturally sensitive? How do we know when we have achieved it? What are the attitudes and behaviors of people who are comfortable and effective working across cultures? How would you recognize such an orientation in teachers and students? In yourself? How can teachers best assist others along this path?

Until relatively recently, little was understood about intercultural development and few benchmarks existed to guide our understanding of how people comprehend cultural difference. The more comprehensive conceptualizations of intercultural effectiveness and sensitivity consider the interaction between the cognitive, affective, and behavioral domains, and teachers must understand this interplay. People with an intercultural mind-set, for instance, move from avoidance or a tolerance of difference to a respect and appreciation of difference. They move from an unconscious ethnocentrism to a more ethnorelative orientation, becoming increasingly aware of their own, as well as others', culture and behavior. Instead of trying to avoid racism, sexism, and other prejudices, such individuals seek out ways to create respectful, productive intercultural relationships. Interculturally effective people are proactive in nature and seek out diverse perspectives and contributions when making decisions and taking actions.

In developing effectiveness across cultures, interculturally effective people strive to acquire a number of skills. They respond to others in a nonjudgmental manner and search for more than one cultural interpretation of behavior or generate multiple attributions and check them out. They also learn to mediate conflicts and solve problems in culturally appropriate ways; promote effective intercultural interactions through mutual adaptation to style differences; model culturally sensitive behaviors and attitudes; and work to institutionalize an intercultural perspective in their personal and professional lives. Ultimately, intercultural competence refers to the maintenance of a vision that stresses the dignity of all cultures as well as the adoption of a skill set that employs intercultural communication in effective and ethical ways.

Interculturally competent individuals are thus able to shift their frame of reference as required, recognize and respond appropriately to cultural differences, listen empathically, perceive others accurately, maintain a nonjudgmental approach to communication, and gather appropriate information about another culture. In real life outside the classroom, such skills are critical when people engage in decision making, negotiation, or problem solving across cultures; when subordinates and authority figures from different backgrounds interact extensively; when individuals or families make major transitions; or when nations and people come together to resolve major differences.

Intercultural education and training, however, is a delicate and difficult endeavor that must be approached with the greatest of sensitivity. Milton Bennett (1993) points out that intercultural interactions among human populations have typically been accompanied by violence and aggression when he states:

> Intercultural sensitivity is not natural. It is not part of our primate past, nor has it characterized most of human history. Cross-cultural contact usually has been accompanied by bloodshed, oppression, or genocide. Education and training in intercultural communication is an approach to changing our "natural" behavior. With the concepts and skills developed in this field, we ask learners to transcend traditional ethnocentrism and to explore new relationships across cultural boundaries. This attempt at change must be approached with the greatest possible care. (p. 21)

Bennett's Developmental Model of Intercultural Sensitivity, or the DMIS, provides a framework for understanding individual development and awareness along a continuum from a highly ethnocentric to a highly ethnorelative perspective. In explaining the DMIS, Bennett notes that an increase in cultural awareness is accompanied by improved cognitive sophistication. Specifically, as people's ability to understand difference increases, so does their ability to negotiate a variety of worldviews.

The DMIS is a six-stage model that describes the experience of cultural difference. By providing a framework for understanding how people develop intercultural sensitivity, it allows educators and trainers to address the question, "What do we do next?" Such a model offers a valuable tool as we work to guide students toward greater cross-cultural sensitivity.

The three stages that lie on the ethnocentric side of the DMIS continuum reflect the tendency of people with limited intercultural experience to exhibit a worldview in which their own culture is central to reality. Three additional stages reflect increasingly ethnorelative perspectives and skills that people exhibit when they experience their own culture in the context of other cultures. The DMIS is a constructivist model, which helps us to better understand the complex phenomenon of culture and intercultural experience as well as the important role experience plays in the attainment of an ethnorelative perspective. As people move through the stages, their worldview becomes increasingly complex.

On the ethnocentric side, an individual may be at the stage of denial, defense, or minimization. On the ethnorelative side, an individual may be at the stage of acceptance, adaptability, or integration.

Denial. Denial refers to the inability to see cultural differences. People in this stage see their own culture as the only real one and have a tendency to isolate or separate themselves in homogeneous groups. Individuals at this stage typically ignore the reality of diversity and often take part in well-meant, but ignorant, stereotyping and superficial statements of tolerance. One can think of the Archie Bunker TV character of the 1970s as a classic example. At this stage, one's construal of difference is minimal, and one attributes cultural difference to a deficiency in intelligence or personality of the other. There is a tendency to dehumanize outsiders, viewing them as simple, undifferentiated aspects or objects of their environment, thus making them easy targets for discrimination, exploitation, or conquer.

When traveling, if they do, people in this stage emphasize familiar categories and just do not see differences. If they are Americans in Tokyo, for instance, they have an "American" experience and may say things like, "Tokyo is like the United States—lots of cars, tall buildings, and McDonald's."

Bennett calls this stage the "stupid questions syndrome." People in denial tend to have a few simple ideas or pieces of stereotypical knowledge about a country or culture. Consider Africa. The stereotypical knowledge many European Americans have of Africa might include wild animals, poverty, black people, and jungle. People in denial will think about everything having to do with Africa, then, in terms of these four ideas. Upon meeting an African, all these images will come to the forefront. Such a person may think or ask, "So, when you leave your hut in the morning, aren't you afraid the wild animals from the jungle will attack you?"

Stop for a moment and ask yourself about the ways many around the world might categorize Americans. Do they tend to see Americans as overweight (lovers of fast food), lazy, rich, and driving big cars? If so, upon meeting an American, such people might ask, "So, when you leave your big house in the morning, do you get in your big car and drive to McDonald's for your big breakfast?" They are bringing forth all of their stereotypical information in their judgment of this American.

The use of stereotypes is quite common in this stage. Stereotyping is one way people's minds work to help simplify the world around them. People tend to categorize information. That is, people put similar pieces of information into common groups or categories in an attempt to bring some sense of order to the complex world in which they live. Stereotypes are merely categories of people; they are socially constructed by a given group to simplify the identification of individuals who are in some way "other."

The term *stereotype* refers to any sort of summary statement or prototypic image that obscures the differences within a group. People have a tendency to view others' behavior as negative and to use this information as trait labels. These negative trait labels then become associated with groups of people, thus becoming negative stereotypes. And because it is oftentimes easier for people to think categorically, the use of negative stereotypes becomes more common than we would like.

The distinction between stereotypes and generalizations is important to consider at this point. A generalization refers to the tendency of a majority of the people in a group to exhibit a certain trait or characteristic. Thus, we could safely say that most people in a group held certain values or shared certain nonverbal communication patterns. Such information can be supported by research documentation and can be applied to a large proportion of a group. Stereotyping, on the other hand, refers to the application of a generalization to every person in that group. Thus, unsupported information blurs specific knowledge about other individuals, and people operate under the assumption that all people in a particular group act in the same way. Because people often have limited and negative stereotypical knowledge, many people interact with others using wrong and sometimes dangerous information.

Individuals in the stage of denial are not capable of thinking about difference and must discover commonalities among people before they can move on. Helping people move from this stage to the next involves helping them develop better skills of discrimination or create other categories, thus becoming more sophisticated in their thinking and more complex in their cognitive processing. When traveling, it becomes the teacher's responsibility to help his or her students see beyond that which is immediately visible and to point out the underlying differences, motivations, and practices that may not be evident on the surface, or objective, level.

Defense. Defense is the next stage of the DMIS. Movement into this stage is driven by the inadequacies of the existing rudimentary categories. Defense is characterized by the recognition of cultural difference, with one's own group seen as the only viable one. The greater the cultural difference observed, the more negative the accompanying evaluation. Strong dualistic "us versus them" thinking is common in this stage, and it is often accompanied by overt negative stereotyping. When forced into contact with others, individuals in this stage tend to become defensive. They feel that people everywhere are all becoming the same, or they see the world as becoming American. While people in this stage are beginning to have a more differentiated view of others, there tends to be a "hardening of the categories" with a narrow focus on a small, typically elite, sample of a society. People thus defend their own way as the one best way.

It's not uncommon for people to be in the defense stage, but they must be encouraged to move on. The developmental tasks at this stage require supporting people affectively while stressing the commonalities among people. When traveling, teachers may need to spend considerable time in one-on-one discussions or small group debriefings with students, gently nudging them on toward the next level.

Minimization. Movement from defense to minimization comes with the discovery of commonality. People in this stage tend to recognize and accept superficial objective cultural differences such as eating customs, money, and so forth, while holding the belief that all human beings are essentially the same. The emphasis at this stage is on the similarity of people and the commonality of basic values, with the tendency to define the basis of commonality in ethnocentric terms. For instance, a person in this stage might think that "since everyone is essentially the same, they're really pretty much like me." This perceived commonality could exist around physical universalism ("We are all the same—we all eat, sleep, breathe, bleed red, and die," or "We are all people of color after all") or around spiritual universalism ("Deep down we are all children of the same God, whether we know it or not").

This is a very profound stage, and there is evidence to suggest that most teachers are at this stage—and they are pleased to be here because they have transcended defense (Mahon 2002). It thus becomes difficult to move people from this stage because they think they are doing OK.

People in this stage see others as basically the same, with little recognition of the differences that do, in fact, exist. People may make reference to physical characteristics—race, for instance—and say that they are not important as long as all people are treated the same. In minimization, people ignore the influence of culture and lived experience that may be quite different between people. There tends to be a belief that all people have the same needs—when in reality they do not.

To help people move out of this stage, one must help them develop cultural self-awareness by pointing out aspects of their own culture and showing them how it might differ relative to another's. However, this does not mean that people must like and accept everything—people can maintain a moral compass by contextualizing another's behavior and beliefs. Take nudity for example. Is it appropriate to take off your clothes? Well, it depends—the context here is critical. In certain circumstances it is appropriate to take off your clothes, as in the shower, but in other circumstance, as out in public, perhaps it is not. The context explains the behavior. Culture thus becomes the context from which to explore another's values. When the context is set (i.e., greeting behavior in Japan), then one decides if he or she will behave according to that context and bow or shake hands. Once this is accepted, the person can move from minimization to acceptance. When traveling with students, it is important for teachers to point out subtle differences in people's experiences, for instance. Having discussions with host nationals about how Americans or others are perceived locally will help to point out the significant differences that do make a difference.

A critical paradigmatic shift in thinking must occur in order for an individual to move into the ethnorelative stages. The individual must stop seeing difference as something to be avoided and begin seeing it as something to be sought out. Individuals in these more advanced stages search for ways to adapt to difference and begin to recognize that people live in culturally different contexts. According to the DMIS model there are three stages on the ethnorelative side: acceptance, adaptation, and integration.

Acceptance. At this stage, the individual begins to demonstrate the ability to interpret phenomena within a cultural context and is better able to analyze complex interactions in culture-contrast terms. People in this stage also begin to seek out cultural difference. While people find that they may not necessarily agree with all they see practiced within another culture, they can, at least, understand the reasons behind what they witness. Student travelers staying with host families in Mexico, for instance, might understand that family or other collective influences may be greater in a Latino culture, and thus better understand why they are expected to be in with the family on most evenings instead of being free to roam the community as they might be back home.

But acceptance alone is not sufficient to drive effectiveness with another culture. The development of new skills in communication and behavior becomes essential.

Adaptation. In the next stage, adaptation, the individual begins to see cultural categories as more flexible and becomes more competent in her or his ability to communicate across cultures. Individuals thus are able to use empathy effectively, to communicate cross-culturally, to shift frames of reference, and to understand others better and be understood across cultural boundaries.

Movement into this stage is driven by a need for action—improving communication skills to build better relations, for instance—and cognitive empathy, the ability to change frames of reference. A significant amount of groundwork must be laid before people are ready to learn new skills and such a shift can occur. The greater the cultural gap, the more difficult it will be to make such a shift. One begins to experience reality in a more "other" way and can understand and have feelings about the world as the other would.

But at this stage people are not simply acquiring skills. Nor are they simply regurgitating lists of dos and don'ts. Knowledge and behavior here are linked by conscious intention, with category boundaries becoming more flexible and permeable, and intentional perspective-taking and empathy occurring.

Integration. The final stage, integration, while rarely achieved, reflects those individuals who have multiple frames of reference and can identify and move rather freely within more than one cultural group. Integration refers to the internalization of bicultural or multicultural frames of reference. Individuals at this level are able to mediate between multiple groups. They tend to maintain a definition of self-identity that is "marginal" to any particular culture and see themselves as "in process," characterized by acceptance of an identity that is not primarily based in any one culture. People at this level are able to facilitate constructive contact between cultures and tend to become cultural mediators or cultural bridges.

This is a rare and difficult level for people to achieve, and it is also difficult to measure. Such skill comes about after significant opportunity for immersion and firsthand interaction over an extended period of time. While the travel experience may provide the vehicle that opens the door for change to occur, it is unlikely that individuals will attain this level without having a significant lived experience within one or more cultures. Thus, travel can set the stage for individuals to develop the confidence, as well as some basic competence and skill, needed to attain these levels of intercultural sensitivity and skill.

Understanding that intercultural development is an evolutionary and not a revolutionary process should greatly influence the manner in which we educate both children and teacher-education students. Intercultural competence is not achieved in one course or one travel experience. Rather, it is important to determine where on the developmental continuum an individual lies and recognize that intercultural competence comes as the result of systematic, oftentimes repetitious, and well-planned exposure to intercultural interactions that are designed to nudge an individual to increasingly complex levels. Moving too quickly along the continuum is akin to the scuba diver plunging immediately to a depth of one hundred feet without taking the requisite time to equalize pressure and accommodate to the new environment—the shock can just be too great for the system to accept. Alternatively, gradual movement or immersion enables one to adjust to the changing circumstances and thus to function more effectively in the new context. So it is with intercultural development. Understanding what we know about intercultural development and sensitivity and integrating it into the education of young people and teachers will result in a more culturally effective and culturally competent citizenry.

6

CHANGE YOUR LATITUDE, CHANGE YOUR ATTITUDE: FACILITATING ADOLESCENT ADJUSTMENT

> No one who has lived through the second half of the twentieth century could possibly be blind to the enormous impact of exchange programs on the future of countries.
>
> —Bill Clinton, 1993

The travel experience can work in two directions—sometimes we are the ones who are traveling, but at other times we play host to international students who come to our schools and live in our communities. Individuals, families, and certainly schools can play host to international exchange students, and all can grow in numerous ways as a result of the experience. It is within the formal educational context that adolescents participate in the majority of international travel and exchange programs. Such programs include structured semester- or year-abroad exchange programs where students live with a host family and attend a local school; formal travel experiences undertaken by a foreign language class or musical group that spends one to two weeks traveling and/or performing abroad; and focused summer experiences. This chapter explores various phases of intercultural adjustment with reference to the adolescent exchange experience in the school context.

The adolescent exchange experience allows participants to learn about a new culture in the same way they learned their original one—by living with a family. As they accommodate cultural differences and struggle to survive and make sense of their new environment, they begin to trust others and ultimately gain a feeling of being at home in another setting.

Cross-cultural adjustment refers to the processes people go through as they begin to understand and adapt to the very real differences they encounter while making a transition to new surroundings. There are, not surprisingly, a number of things to which people must adjust when they encounter a foreign culture, and these things are experienced at both the objective and the subjective levels. Early in an experience, one must make numerous adjustments to physical differences in the environment—new foods that are eaten, the systems of work or study that are encountered, the ways people use transportation, and so forth. People must also adjust to differences in the ways people interact with one another, and may confront significant differences in value and belief systems. Here, individuals may begin to wrestle with their own commitment and willingness to make changes in their manner of thinking and acting. Later on, one may begin to experience significant internal change in terms of intercultural identity and development—just the steps needed to advance toward more ethnorelative stages of intercultural sensitivity.

Numerous models of cross-cultural adjustment have been proposed over the years that are designed to provide sojourners with some sense of what they might expect to encounter as they experience a cross-cultural transition. The one that resonates most with people is commonly referred to as the *U-curve hypothesis* (Lysgaard 1955; Trifonovitch 1977). This hypothesis suggests that people experience four phases throughout their adjustment, and these phases have been given some rather clever names. Imagine the letter U with four spots identified along the letter.

The *honeymoon* phase occurs early in the experience at the top left of the U. Here, everything is new and exciting—there are new foods to eat, new people to meet, and new sights to see. There can also be new ways of getting around town, and people might look forward to giving up their dependence upon the automobile, using public transportation, and mingling with the locals.

Characterized by exhilaration, discovery, and anticipation, this rather euphoric stage doesn't last long. Soon, people find that the demands of setting up a new home and learning how to function in the new setting take their emotional toll. It *is* stressful to settle into a new place, and one's body doesn't differentiate good stress from bad stress—it just reacts to the sudden flow of adrenaline in the system. People thus cannot remain in this euphoric state for long.

The next phase, *hostility*, is then experienced as one moves down the left side toward the bottom of the U. After some time, one's behavior doesn't bring about the expected results; one can't get one's favorite foods, toiletries, or "a good cup of coffee." Or, while it may have been initially exciting to get around town as the locals do, the fact that the public transportation system never seems to run on time, causing people to be late for appointments, begins to be bothersome. People can become quite frustrated, angry, or depressed. Individuals have two choices here. They can either put on their ethnocentric hat and go home, where they believe "things are done the correct way," or they can remain and begin to learn how other people do things from their own cultural perspective. This is when true culture learning begins to take place. Here, the fact that people are often late is not taken as being inconsiderate or insensitive, but it is understood that an emphasis on time may not be the same for all people. In some contexts a person may come to a meeting any time after the set appointment and not be considered late; the important thing is that the meeting occurred.

If a person stays and begins to learn effectively, he or she emerges from the bottom of the U and enters a state that is often referred to as *humor*. This stage suggests that as people learn more culturally appropriate behavior they can begin to laugh at how they might have looked to locals when they first arrived. It is a good sign, and it suggests that one is well on the way to adjustment.

Finally, people enter a state called *home* as they reach the top of the U and can now see the world from two equally valid perspectives. People are thought to be in this state when they are well adjusted and bicultural. It can take up to two years for people to make a full and complete cultural adjustment and to arrive at the top of the U—a significant amount of time, and this is with full immersion.

Building upon this idea, other researchers proposed the W *hypothesis*, extending the initial U-curve of adjustment to include the return to one's home culture (Gullahorn and Gullahorn 1963). People find that when they return home after an extended time away, there is often an unexpected readjustment or reentry shock to being home. It can be quite difficult to integrate one's new learning and perspectives into one's life when others have not had similar experiences and similar growth.

These are easy and convenient models for people to adopt, and it is not uncommon for a student to approach a teacher saying something like, "I think I need to talk to you. I feel like I'm at the bottom of my U." Such a model makes intuitive sense and is easy for people to remember. Unfortunately there has been little tangible evidence that either of these models, in fact, operate as they were originally proposed. They are just not well supported in the recent research literature.

Since these initial hypotheses were proposed, more comprehensive analyses of the adjustment process have been undertaken by a number of other researchers (Pedersen 1995; Ward, Bochner, and Furnham 2001). Regardless of the model used to describe the process of adjustment, something influential does happen during a sojourn—it may just not be as easy to document and explain in a neat little image as was suggested by the early models. However, adjustment can be thought of as an ongoing process that is generally experienced in five general phases, including predeparture preparation, arrival and settling in, culture shock, culture learning where relationships are built, and reentry.

Predeparture. Predeparture preparation, at least for the overseas exchange experience, includes the period of time from when an individual completes an application to when he or she has been accepted and ultimately placed with a host family. For the class preparing to travel overseas, it begins from the moment students, teachers, and families hear about the possibility that they may travel overseas, as when my students began preparing for the Belizean adventure months before our actual sojourn.

The predeparture stage is typically characterized by excitement, anticipation, new discovery, and positive perceptions. As departure time nears, the student is busy saying good-bye to family and friends, shopping for last-minute items, and perhaps sending a letter of introduction off to a prospective host family. The host family, too, is usually busy preparing to welcome a new member to the family. This is also a time when students *should* begin preparation for the cross-cultural exchange and interaction that is certain to occur; but this is seldom the case. It seems to be difficult for most prospective sojourners to anticipate the kinds of communication problems, cross-cultural misunderstandings, and other potential pitfalls they will encounter, and many just do not pay much attention at this time to issues related to culture and adjustment.

This is one of the ironies of cross-cultural orientation and one of the counterintuitive findings in the research. Few people, especially those who have not traveled before, tend to pay much attention to cross-cultural issues during predeparture orientation sessions. It is generally not until they arrive at their destination and begin to have some concrete experiences that may not make sense that people begin to question the reality of their new environment and express an interest in cross-cultural issues. Most tend to be too caught up in the excitement of leaving to attend to such "academic" issues.

> A number of years ago, after returning to Ohio following four years living and studying in Hawaii, our family decided to host a visiting high school exchange student. Already quite involved with AFS Intercultural Programs through my dissertation study in New Zealand, as well as knowing that our local AFS community group was quite active and supportive, we applied to host a student. We reviewed papers of a few potential female applicants who were interested in a year in the United States. Yuzuki's application stood out among the rest for our family. Coming from the island of Kyushu in Japan, Yuzuki described herself as interested in being a "big sister," eager to become active with a variety of different things during her stay in America, a musician who played classical piano, and quiet and reserved.
>
> That she was—when she arrived. After a year with us, Yuzuki returned home to play drums in an Irish rock-and-roll band, subsequently marrying an Irishman (although they have since divorced). We continue to remain in close contact with Yuzuki and have visited one another since she returned home, and Hyla provided advice and guidance to her via e-mail throughout her pregnancy and the birth of her first child. To say that the experience had an impact on her life would be an understatement. The same could be said for us as a family.
>
> Our first personal contact with Yuzuki came during her predeparture stage the preceding summer. We wanted to initiate some correspondence with her before her arrival. Still homesick for Hawaii, I had arranged to teach summer school classes at the University of Hawaii, planning to

spend the best part of a summer there with my family. We wrote a letter to Yuzuki introducing ourselves and letting her know how much we were looking forward to having her stay with us. If she wished to write us back, we would be at a given address in Honolulu through mid-August.

A few weeks into our stay in Hawaii we received a response from Japan, addressed to where we were staying—in "Honoruru, Hawaii"! And to top things off, Yuzuki informed us in the letter that her mother ran an English language school and that she had spent quite a number of years studying English. This was our first introduction to the kinds of learning and growth experiences that were to occur for all of us as the year progressed. This was also our first taste of the reality of disconfirmed expectations—especially from one who was actively learning English. Oh, what else might we expect?

It wasn't long after Yuzuki arrived in our home that we all began to realize that there were problems in adjustment. But this was not only happening to Yuzuki; it was happening to others as well—other exchange students and families, local kids in the school, and the teachers. Good exchange programs are characterized by supportive networks of community volunteers, host families, and host schools who come together to ease the adjustment shock, or culture shock, the student is certain to experience. It is not uncommon for these school and community support groups to host regular gatherings designed to allow international students, their host families, and teachers to discuss their experiences—both the joys as well as the frustrations. It can be quite enlightening for all as they began to learn more and more about each other's cultures and the cross-cultural experience.

Arrival and Settling In. Arrival and settling in can actually span a rather lengthy period of time as students initially integrate into a new family and community and ultimately become included in a new school. While students may feel comfortable and at home in some settings, they are constantly being introduced to others where they are exposed to countless new stimuli. When the novelty of the experience begins to wear off, it may feel like the host culture is beginning to intrude on the visitor's life. This stage is often characterized by confusion, self-blame, tension, frustration, loss, depression, and withdrawal. One's emotions can become quite engaged, and physical symptoms such as headaches and stomach pains may occur.

In many ways, the exchange student experience is similar to that of many other sojourners. However, there are some significant differences. For one, the student is generally on her or his own. That is, while students may travel to their host country with a group of fellow nationals, usually within a few days of arriving they are matched up with their host family, and off they go. After the initial arrival into a new country the process of settling in begins, with the sojourner experiencing many new and unexpected things. It is not uncommon for new sojourners to have the sense that things, or people for that matter, all seem to look alike. Because so much is new and different, and the stimuli are in most cases not what one has been accustomed to, it is difficult to distinguish details, and things pretty much blend together. Developing an insider's perspective and the ability to differentiate the finer differences between individuals takes some time and familiarity. Outsiders just don't see most of the detail and thus miss out on much until they have been around for a longer period of time. Extended immersion in a new context provides the time one needs to learn to focus on the new details and begin to make sense of the new environment.

When entering a new country and/or interacting within a new cultural setting for the first time, the sojourner confronts another surprise—how powerfully his or her emotions are aroused (Cushner and Brislin 1996). People expect there to be objective, or physical, differences across cultures. What they often don't expect is the degree to which their own emotions will be engaged, and how this will impact their initial adjustment.

Exchange students and their host families eagerly anticipate the arrival and initial meeting that will take place, each having some expectation of how those awkward "getting-to-know-you" moments will unfold. It is from this first moment when people greet one another that emotions are high, and the ambiguity of the cross-cultural encounter and the reality of cultural differences become evident. A number of emotional experiences occur in the early stages of a sojourn, as a result of confronting disconfirmed expectations, experiencing a certain degree of anxiety and ambiguity, and feeling a need to belong and "fit in." Rosa's host mother shared this story of her first encounter with Rosa, when they greeted her at the airport upon her arrival from the Dominican Republic.

CHAPTER 6

We all waited in excited anticipation for the plane to taxi from the runway. All of us, that is, except my husband, as he couldn't get off work to come to the airport. But I was there with my kids: Roger, our twelve-year-old son, and Lisa, our fourteen-year-old daughter. As people were getting off the plane, we all ran over toward the doorway holding our "Welcome Rosa" sign as well as a few balloons and streamers we had brought. You know, kind of what you'd expect to welcome someone new. We had our photo of Rosa with us so we would recognize her when she got off the plane. And we recognized her right away; she had this big grin on her face as she walked toward us. I introduced myself to her and then introduced the kids. She smiled, let out a big "hola," and proceeded to kiss each of us on the cheek. I didn't quite know what to do, and was kind of at a loss when she offered her face to me. We all kind of stood there, quite astonished! And the kids! Well, they didn't stop talking about that for a week. They never expected to kiss anyone they really didn't know, especially the first time they met. I warned my husband that this might happen before he got home so he wouldn't be as shocked as we were. But it didn't. I guess Rosa learned pretty fast that we don't kiss one another when we first meet.

That is the essence of the cross-cultural encounter: people go about their business as they normally would but unintentionally offend the other. As you can imagine, Rosa saw the same situation somewhat differently. Rosa shared her perception of the same experience with the other students; and she felt as if her host family really didn't want her.

When I arrived I was all excited and happy to meet my new family. I had been up half the night on the plane, unable to sleep, I was so excited. When we finally arrived, I gathered my stuff, walked off the plane, saw that wonderful welcome sign the family had made, and ran up to give my new family a kiss. That's how we greet at home; it's only natural to kiss people when you meet, especially among women. And you expect one in return. Well, when this didn't happen I thought the family really didn't want me. I could sense that something was wrong. Perhaps they had been forced to take an exchange student, I didn't know. I was really uncomfortable at first and didn't quite know what to do. It took a day or two until we could talk about this as a family. Now I understand that Americans just don't kiss like we do. They are much more formal in their interactions with others. I guess shaking hands helps to keep people at a comfortable distance, I don't know.

Good cross-cultural training strives to result in both people in the interaction making the same judgment about the other or at least being able to understand and explain an encounter in the same way. The technical term used by psychologists is *isomorphic attributions*; or making judgments about the other person similar to those that the person would make about himself or herself. In Rosa's case, both she and her host family would have understood the greeting behavior of the other and made similar judgments about one another.

Greeting behaviors can occur for quite some time and in a variety of contexts for exchange students, even after the initial welcome is long past. Mr. Thompson, the drama teacher, shared an incident that happened with his students when he took them on an outing at the beginning of the year. This also pointed out the ambiguity that can surround greeting behavior.

> At the start of each year I like to take my students to a community theater to see a play. This is my way of having my students begin to look at drama and theater; viewing a full program so the students can then study the various dimensions of a production. We look at everything, from acting, costuming, prop construction, lighting and other behind-the-scenes work, and even marketing. After the production, we went backstage to talk with the stage crew. While there, I happened to run into a woman, Mrs. Carroll, an older African American woman. She and I used to volunteer with one another on similar community productions. We hadn't seen each other for about five years and were obviously quite happy to see one another. Mrs. Carroll, I must tell you, is a very warm woman, and as sweet as can be. When we saw each other, we approached one another and embraced with a big hug. I guess I didn't think too much about this, although in retrospect, perhaps I should have.
>
> The next day there was quite a bit of snickering and small talk when I walked into class. I asked the students what all the excitement was about. One of the more vocal students, Carol, said they were just talking about the outing. She was still giggling as she went on to say that Franci, our international student from Austria, had asked if the black woman was my wife or girlfriend. I really was amazed that this could have been taken that way. But I guess now I understand it; we did greet each other rather warmly. We went on to have a brief discussion comparing relationship and greeting behavior in the United States and Austria. We all enjoyed a few laughs together, and learned quite a bit as well.

Mrs. James, one of the high school counselors, is the faculty adviser to the international student group. In this capacity she interacts with students in a number of ways, helping them get settled into school, linking them up with American students who serve as mentors, and just being there as a general support for students in need. She related an incident that had happened a year earlier on one of the first days of school as she welcomed two new immigrant students from Vietnam.

> These kids had been in the country only a short time and were new to our school. I needed to administer a placement test to them so I would know which math class to put them in. They were sitting in the office waiting area when I came out, ready to take them to the library where they could take their test in some quiet space. I gestured to them with my arm as I said something like, "Come with me to the library so you can take the placement test." As I called to them I felt a sudden panic—they weren't coming with me. I waved harder, smiled bigger, and spoke louder and slower. Still nothing.
>
> In retrospect, I understand how my words said one thing but my body said something totally different. You see, in their culture, as with many from Southeast Asia, having the palm upward with the fingers moving toward you is an insult. This is a gesture one would use to call a dog or someone in a lower status than you. At that moment, I was belittling and downgrading them. No wonder they weren't following me—I had inadvertently insulted them. I should have gestured with my palm toward the ground with my fingers moving toward me. This may have been a simple error, and I certainly did not mean to offend anyone, but it sure carried a strong, negative message. I wonder how often that happens, especially early in relationships between people?

Another common occurrence in the cross-cultural exchange is that people's expectations are not met. And again, it is not that people are ill-mannered or inconsiderate—some things are just not anticipated. The Anderson family shared their experience when Seiko came to live with them from Japan.

> A few weeks after Seiko arrived we were able to discuss with her how she felt when she first settled into our home. It certainly was not as we had expected! We thought that from the very beginning we went to all extremes to make her feel a part of our home and family. Our family life was rather

busy at the time. Although we thought of ourselves otherwise, we probably weren't much different from many other American families with young children. We seemed to constantly be on the run between both of our work schedules that included some evening meetings or teaching, getting our children off to school in the morning, making sure they got home afterward to go to soccer practice, music, and dance lessons, and visiting parents an hour away on a weekly basis. And, to top it off, we had just bought our first house and were preparing to move within six weeks of Seiko's arrival. Yet, through all this, we wanted Seiko to just feel comfortable, be as one of the family, and fit right into our schedule. In fact, we expected that our approach would help, so we did as most American families would do. In the first days we showed Seiko where everything was in the house, taught her how to operate various appliances so she could cook herself a meal if she was hungry before we all got home, and told her to make herself at home and to do whatever she wanted.

Well, in talking to Seiko a few weeks into her stay we quickly found out how awkward all of this made her feel. She was quite uncomfortable helping herself to food in the cupboard or refrigerator and doing things like operating the washing machine or sitting down to watch television alone. We prided ourselves on treating Seiko as one of the family. She, on the other hand, thought of us as unfriendly and felt rejected, expecting us to treat her as a special guest, especially in the first weeks after her arrival.

Here we have a classic case of disconfirmed expectations experienced by both Seiko and her host family. People tend to have certain expectations of what a new place or situation will be like, as well as how they will function in the process. The reality of the situation, however, can often be quite different from what one initially expected. What one expects to find may not, in fact, materialize. Reconciling the difference between the dream and the reality is necessary if people are to make good cross-cultural adjustments. Sojourners must come to grips with the reality of where they find themselves or they will withdraw deeper into a culture shock that can color their subsequent experience.

Culture Shock. The next phase, often referred to as culture shock, occurs when the individual becomes quite confused, oftentimes disregarding both the similarities and the differences between the host culture and the home culture. This stage, too, can be highly emotional and is often characterized by hostility, defensive behavior, a feeling of vulnerability, rebellion, blame, and rejection of all that the host culture represents.

Many of the reasons for this culture shock are related to some of the emotional issues discussed earlier. However, once the initial settling in has occurred, more significant cultural differences become evident and can be the cause of more complex problems. It is here that real culture learning occurs.

One aspect that new students must attend to early in their experience is that of language. Once the jet lag has diminished and the student has learned his or her way around a new home and neighborhood, it is essential to begin tuning one's ear to the local language. Where the languages spoken are different and one is building competence in the new tongue, one is also building trust and understanding between oneself and other significant people. Even when the local language is the same as that spoken by the student back home, which is the case for those moving within English-speaking countries, a considerable amount of new vocabulary may not translate, may be used in a very different manner, may be spoken with a new accent, or may be accompanied by nonverbal expressions that are either poorly understood or misinterpreted. When the same language is spoken, it is also possible that people may feel comfortable and familiar with one another before a deep and trusting relationship has actually been established, thus bringing student, family, and teachers into potentially difficult situations.

Jean, an American student who had spent the previous year in a school in Queensland, Australia, was serving as a local peer counselor to new exchange students. She had a very important role, especially early in the school year. During one of the orientation sessions that took place about a month after the new students arrived she related the following story. It was her attempt to help these new students feel more comfortable by sharing an experience she had early in her sojourn.

> Australians are much more aware of the subtle language differences that exist between Australian English and American English than I was, especially during my first months in the country. I knew about some pronunciation differences that existed between Australian and American English—such words as tomato and aluminum are pronounced differently, for instance. There are certain "Australianisms" that one comes across as well that are fairly common, like "fair-dinkum," meaning honest or legitimate, and "ta" instead of thanks. Likewise, I was aware that different vocabulary

existed for many words—"bonnet" for the hood of a car, "boot" for its trunk, or "jumper" for what I generally refer to as a sweater. Then there are some terms that one had better not use. You don't "root" for a team down under like we do at home; you "barrack" for the team. To root means to have sexual intercourse, and accidentally asking someone who they root for can get you some pretty strange looks.

There were also different terms used for some common school supplies. At the beginning of the semester the teacher would read a list of required school supplies: pencils, byro, which is their term for a pen, paper, notepads, and so forth. I eagerly wrote this list down in each class on my first day, feeling somewhat like a kindergarten child on their first day of school. In biology class I had this young, rather cute teacher, who seemed to kind of flirt with me when my host sister introduced us at the beginning of class. I was looking forward to being in his class. He proceeded to do the same as the other teachers and read his list: pencils, byros, paper, and rubbers. Rubbers? I had no idea what he could have been talking about. The only rubbers I knew of my grandfather put over his shoes during the winter, and the other, well, I didn't even want to consider it at the moment. I was really thrown by that one. I finally had to ask my host sister what it meant, but I waited until we got home that night—I was too embarrassed to ask anyone in school—even her. Boy did we have a laugh when I learned that "rubbers" refers to pencil erasers! I then could go on and enjoy the rest of the semester with this teacher.

So my message to all relatively new exchange students is to ask questions early when confused or when something is not understood. It oftentimes is a rather innocent difference that can be explained quite simply. Language plays a critical role in adjustment, and the sooner one becomes competent in it, the easier the transition will be.

I shared with the group one of my own experiences that also was related to language and occurred in Australia. This incident points out the difficulty people can have communicating across accents.

Throughout much of the 1970s, Australia was recruiting planeloads of American teachers to fill badly needed vacancies in many of their schools. Not able to let an opportunity go by, Hyla and I went through the interview process and, two days later, were offered a contract. We were married six weeks later and, one week after that, departed for a two-year teaching stint down under.

We met many other young American teachers at the time and became quite close to Barb and Terry, another young couple from Seattle. We shared many things together over the course of the two years: an interest in photography, travel during the school holidays, and we both gave birth to our first child while there.

Few of us had telephones in our homes, especially early in our experience, so we often left messages for each other at our respective schools. One day, Terry received a message at his school that was quite ambiguous, causing him some embarrassment as well as some confusion. The secretary left a note in his mailbox one day that he was to return a call to "Hare Krishna." The word quickly got out among the other teachers, and many were talking behind his back about "this new Yankee teacher who was a member of the Krishna Consciousness movement." Terry was totally confused by this message and bothered by the reaction of his peers as he began getting the cold shoulder from many on staff. It wasn't until the next weekend when we asked Terry why he hadn't returned our phone call that he figured out the problem. My wife, Hyla Cushner, had telephoned the school and left a message for Terry to return her call. The secretary, unaccustomed to an American accent, heard the voice say "Hare Krishna." Mystery solved.

But spoken language is not the only aspect of communication that sojourners must work to understand. A significant amount of our communication takes place on a nonverbal level. In this instance, Ibrahim, from Turkey, was quite offended and wary on the first day in his art class—the result of a misinterpretation of a nonverbal message.

> I was in my art class on the first day when our teacher asked us to make a collage about our experiences during the summer. It wasn't much, just to take a few photos from various magazines that kind of captured what we had done or how we felt. We were to try to communicate our experience to others and to see how they might interpret what we created. I wasn't quite sure how to begin, or really what to do for that matter. The teacher saw me, and I must have looked rather confused. She came over and handed me a pair of scissors, telling me that I should begin cutting from the magazine. Well, I was quite shocked and I'm afraid I might have offended my teacher. You see, in Turkey, we never hand someone a knife or scissors. I guess it goes back to times when not everybody could be trusted. We always place knives or scissors on a table or somewhere in full view and let the other person pick them up themselves. When the teacher handed

me the scissors I had an immediate gut reaction and pulled away in horror. I think I may have startled the teacher as much as she startled me.

Rosa and her teachers constantly had problems related to eye contact. Interculturally skilled people suspend judgment and check out their assumptions when they initially observe certain behavior before making a judgment about a child. As Rosa says,

> Every child in my country, and in the whole Latin American region for that matter, knows that a person shows respect and courtesy to another person, especially teachers and others in authority, by lowering their eyes while interacting with them. It is especially necessary for a child to do this if they have done something wrong. This tells the other person that they are aware of their incorrect behavior.
>
> I now know that here, in the United States, one is often considered guilty or devious if they look away from a person of authority. And I didn't know that it is considered honest or straightforward to look someone in the eyes. And to be honest, I'm still a bit uncomfortable doing this. But I know I have to or other people have the wrong impression of me. Until I realized this I was bothered whenever my teachers would tell me to look at them. And I know they were bothered by my behavior. I wonder how many young children this becomes a problem for in American schools—especially if teachers aren't aware of it. I'll bet a certain number of immigrant children, for instance, might be assumed to be guilty of something just because they are quiet and not looking directly at a teacher. And this seems to be such a simple example. I also wonder what other nonverbal messages are misinterpreted by teachers and students.

Culture Learning. It is in this stage that relationships have begun to crystallize and more meaningful culture learning can take place. While the time required to reach this phase varies depending on any number of factors (family support, individual coping strategies, linguistic competence, degree of cultural gap, etc.), it is here that significant culture learning begins to occur. Likened to the "bottom of the U curve," this is the point where people begin to understand another's perspective and more accurate attributions about behaviors begin to occur. Key to success at this phase is the interpersonal relationships that develop. When safe, supportive, and trusting relationships have formed, be they with host families, local friends, or teachers, people begin to open up, expose their inner feelings and thoughts, and more freely inquire about many of the questions and concerns they may have. This was evident in Yuzuki's interactions with our daughter Shannon, who was thirteen years old at the time. Yuzuki explains it as follows:

> I am the youngest daughter in my family, and with that comes certain expectations. My older sister, too, has certain things that are expected of her. I was quite excited when I learned that I would be staying with a family that had two daughters—both younger than me. I always wanted to be a big sister and have younger sisters look up to me. I think I have quite a bit I can offer them. But now, in retrospect, I don't think that's what Shannon had in mind. And it took a few weeks until this was clear to all of us.
>
> When I first arrived, we shared a bedroom. I was on my best behavior—my mother told me to pick up after myself, help out around the house, and to be a good model for my new sisters. Well, I think I may have overdone it a bit. I tried to give all kinds of advice to Shannon—about who she should spend her time with, to make sure to do her homework, how she should speak to her parents—all the things my sister talked to me about back home in Japan. Well, this didn't go over too well with Shannon, and she got quite angry with me. I was in tears and didn't know what to do. I thought about going home or changing families, it was so awkward.
>
> When we finally talked about it as a family it became clear to me that young Americans Shannon's age want their own independence and are just beginning to step out on their own. They seem to fight quite often with their parents. And here I was, trying to be a mother to her; exactly what she wanted to do without. No wonder she got so mad at me. It also became clear that while I assumed I was to be a big sister, Shannon had always been the big sister in the family and resented me trying to take her role. We can laugh about it now, but I really learned a lot about American teenagers and families through that experience.

Reentry. Regardless of the length of time one has been overseas, returning home can bring a mix of excitement and joy, but also reluctance and dismay. On the one hand, students are anxious to return to family and friends they have missed and to share with others all that they have encountered and learned. On the other hand, they may not want to give up the fun, excitement, and new learning that an overseas experience inevitably brings and return to the "normalcy" of their home culture. This ambivalence is to be expected and will differ depending upon the individual and the kind of experience in which the student participated. For those who spent most of their overseas time with fellow nationals or on a brief study tour, the return home may be easy since they really did not enter the host culture to any degree of depth. For some, if the experience is followed up and built upon after the return home, or for those who have fully entered another culture for a significant length of time, reentry into one's home culture can be more severe an adjustment than the initial culture shock experience, primarily because one has not anticipated the changes he or she has gone through—and it is so unexpected.

The traveler has usually had such an incredibly enriching experience, has changed in so many ways, and is eager to share the new understandings with family and friends once he or she returns home. Most of those who remain at home, however, have not had similar experiences and thus have a difficult time relating to the changed returnee. While the sojourner has changed dramatically, family and friends typically have not. It is not uncommon for returnees to find that others lose interest rather quickly in hearing about their overseas encounters and in seeing photographs of their new friends. While the return traveler may be welcomed home with open arms, she or he is often met with closed eyes and ears.

Many find that it is more difficult to return home than it was to make the initial adjustment to the new culture. Although the individual who went overseas expects to come home a changed person, those who remained at home do not expect this person to be any different. Entering a phase that can be very similar to the initial culture shock, returning travelers may feel as if *home* were new and different. The returnee may feel as if he or she were a stranger in his or her own home; he or she may feel out of place, alienated, alone, or unable to fit in and may have significant difficulty communicating with friends. Some of the social difficulties encountered include having to deal with stereotypes, uncertainty over cultural identity, and social withdrawal (Ward, Bochner, and Furnham 2001). Such is the nature of reentry shock, and that is why it is so important to be prepared for this unexpected inevitability.

Reentry or reverse culture shock can be attributed to a number of possible causes (Austin 1986; Wang 1997; Martin and Harrell 2004). First, there can be a challenge to one's self-concept. Even before individuals return to their home culture, they may become aware that they are not the same as they were before they left home and that significant changes may have occurred. Their sense of identity with a particular country may have changed, or they may have acquired new nonverbal as well as verbal communication behaviors. Returnees may not identify with the same groups they did prior to their experience, or they may not agree with the values of a given group any longer, including, perhaps, their own family. Until they find their new niche back home, and often a new peer group, they may feel quite out of sorts.

Second, returnees must often reconcile any number of disconfirmed expectations, beginning with the realization that they may feel like a foreigner in their own home. If people have been away for a significant period of time, they may have difficulty readjusting to traditional foods or keeping abreast of conversations since local knowledge and attitudes may have changed. While away, the traveler often builds an idealized vision of home—of spending time at favorite places, eating missed foods, visiting with special friends, and so forth. The stage is then set for an enormous letdown when things they return to do not live up to what was expected. Returnees quickly find that relationships have changed and people do not need to hear about the overseas experiences, seeming to be more interested in local gossip.

Others, too, may have equally unrealistic expectations of the returnee and thus confront their own disconfirmed expectations. Family and friends may become upset that the returnee seems critical of home or that she or he does not seem happy. People at home often become confused or upset that the returnee does not seem as interested in local happenings and sometimes may not be able to fully understand what people are talking about. And loved ones may become impatient with returnees who want to continually share their international experience, feeling that they are unwilling to "get back to normal."

Third, there is often a sense of loss. When people return home they are oftentimes leaving people and a way of life that they have grown to love, having to say good-bye to people they may never see again. They may have to give up a lifestyle they have cherished. And students on exchange programs may have enjoyed a special status or identity while abroad, being the focus of people's curiosity and interest. Many may miss certain day-to-day amenities they have come to appreciate, such as efficient mass transportation systems or low-cost public health services.

Finally, perhaps the greatest challenge facing returnees, especially those who have been away for a significant period of time, is that of finding an appropriate way to integrate their international experiences into the day-to-day realities of their home culture. Successful returnees work to identify those changes in their own values and attitudes that are most worth integrating into their life now that they are at home. At the same time, a fine line must often be drawn between what the returnee wishes to try to change in others and what he or she is willing to keep to the self.

Understanding and addressing issues of reentry may be the most critical phase in integrating the goals of the international experience and should really begin from the moment of initial trip planning. After all, it is really the postexperience impact and change on the individual that is the ultimate purpose of engaging in an international sojourn. An expected outcome, thus, is to see growth along the Developmental Model of Intercultural Sensitivity, with individuals moving toward more complex levels of ethnorelativity, becoming less ethnocentric in the ways they interact with others in the world. The goal ultimately for the international experience is that it will have had such a significant impact on the individual that upon his or her return home, he or she has greater understanding of the world and subsequently does things differently in his or her everyday personal or work life. Considering this from the outset helps to remind us that while the actual experience is exciting, it is what we do with the new attitudes, knowledge, and skills that is of most importance. It also helps teachers to extend the learning beyond the orientation and actual trip.

7

LEARNING TO LIVE TOGETHER: BRIDGING INTERCULTURAL BOUNDARIES WITH YOUTH DIALOGUE

> One of the higher callings for young people in the coming century will be working to increase intercultural understanding. Such people will be the missionaries of the age, spreading light among groups . . . by giving them a modern vision of the new global community.
>
> —Carl Coon

"We've been struggling in our region with misperception, miscommunication, hate, violence, and war for decades," Mohammed began, speaking to a group of American young people at a summer program in California. "Each time one person is attacked in Israel or Palestine there is retribution from the other side. Violence in each case leads to more violence—and a vicious cycle is established that never seems to end. Aren't we sick of this already?"

Then he posed the most profound question to his young students. "How many of you are willing to put aside your preconceived ideas about others and listen to the other—I mean really take the time to listen to one another? Can you listen to their pain? Because it's there on both sides of this conflict. We're all hurting, and for some reason people think that retribution will reduce their pain. Unfortunately that only leads to more violence, and we all lose."

Mohammed sat back and let his words sink in for a while. The young people in this particular group were quiet and contemplative, as the heat of the day, as well as of the moment, simmered through the group. It was, after all, relatively early in the summer experience, only the second week of the camp. These young people were just beginning to get to know one another. After a long pause, Stephan finally spoke.

"I know when I was growing up in California," he offered, "I had very limited understanding of the conflict in the Middle East. I was raised in a Jewish community where I was taught that we were the good guys and we wore the white hats, and everyone else, meaning the Arabs, were the bad guys, and they wore the black hats. I'm sorry to say that I didn't even know who the Palestinians were. I was told that I could not trust people in the Arab community. I'm really glad to have the opportunity to learn firsthand from all of you what the reality of your lives is like."

"I feel really ignorant about your situation and rather guilty because I know so little," added Sarah, a sixteen-year-old camper who lived outside Washington, D.C. "In the United States, we're somewhat protected from the pains and struggles of many of the world's people and don't have much of a clue about what's going on. I know many people stereotype others quite a lot. This camp experience is helping me to understand that all Arabs are not this way and all Jews are not that way. There's quite a bit of ignorance, but I do believe interest among Americans is changing. I'm beginning to get embarrassed by the way most of us act."

"I am told that I cannot trust Jews anywhere in the world," Rema interjected. "I grew up in East Jerusalem, and my family, and entire community for that matter, filled me with stories of the atrocities that were directed toward our people simply because we were Palestinian. Some members of my family were shot during a recent confrontation in Jerusalem. Now I'm considered a traitor by some in my community for wanting to spend time with this mixed group of Arabs, Jews, and Americans in the United States. They tell me that I cannot trust the motivations of most of you. That's what I'm struggling with right now. I want things to be different, but it's so hard."

Ibrahim, a young student from the West Bank town of Hebron, spoke next. "My major concern and reason for coming to the United States was to be a spokesman for my people. You are the future leaders of this country," he said, as he focused his gaze upon the Americans in the group. "Some of you will be judging my future, or my people's future, some day. I want you to be informed so you are able to see all sides of a problem or situation."

There was a lull in the conversation as Mohammed scanned the group. Looking around at one another, many were fidgeting and obviously uncomfortable.

"I heard the same things from my parents that Rema heard in her home," added Schmuel, an Israeli Jewish student from Rishon le Zion, a suburb of Tel Aviv. "It wasn't until I was in high school and we spent a week at Neve Shalom that I began to seriously question what I was hearing at home and in my community. Until recently I wanted all Arabs out of Israel. I thought that there was no way possible that we would ever be able to live side by side. I now think that it may be possible, although I don't quite know how! It's very frustrating and scary; especially at the moment."

"What's Neve Shalom?" asked Natalie, a young Quaker participant from Chicago. "And why did it give you such hope?"

"Neve Shalom is a joint Arab–Jewish community comprised of equal numbers of Arab families and Jewish families who are devoted to living together and learning one another's language, religion, and culture," replied Schmuel. "There are about thirty families who live in the community, midway between Tel Aviv and Jerusalem. They also offer workshops and opportunities for outsiders to learn about their efforts and to explore the possibility of coexistence. I found it an extremely valuable and worthwhile experiment. Me and some friends from my high school spent a week there last year. That experience really inspired us and left me with a lot to think about."

"Why do you think people are so afraid of trying and of trusting one another?" asked Mohammed. "And what do you think can be done to change things?"

Again there was silence, the questions seemingly as profound and as troubling as the situation itself.

"Again," Stephan offered, "I may be rather naive, but it seems to me that just doing what we're doing here today is a beginning. I know in my school when there is conflict between, say, blacks and whites, teachers try to get both parties to sit down and talk about their differences. It doesn't always work, but at least it's an effort."

"But it doesn't work like that in the region," Rema interjected, obviously becoming upset. "It seems rather simplistic from your point of view, I suppose; why people don't just begin to talk to one another. But you don't understand the stress that we live under, the histories of our people and their experiences with one another. Back home, we don't go to school with one another—we have separate schools for Jews and Arabs. And we don't live in the same communities like you do in the United States.

"I realize that here in the United States you have your tensions too, but they are different. Maybe young people in America worry about their parents getting divorced; they live among others who use drugs; they worry about what to study in college or who to date. I understand these are all stressors. Young people all over the world live under stress; but they are stressors of a different kind. I don't think you can truly understand the tensions we live under without experiencing it yourself. And I also understand, I think, the stress that Schmuel lives with. As an Israeli, both he and I know that when he returns home he will join the military and will probably be dispatched to the West Bank and have his weapons aimed at my people. How should I feel when I am here with him?"

She paused. "Schmuel, what *will* you do? I wish things were different. It is all very confusing." Rema sighed, as if she had been waiting to say something like this for a long time.

Schmuel was speechless, and a silence once again fell over the group.

And so began the exploration, introspection, shift in perspective, and bridge building that unfolded, layer by layer, as these young Americans struggled to gain a deeper understanding of the range of issues that face their peers in other countries while trying to develop trust in one another. Over time in such an environment these young people grow in their understanding and appreciation of the tensions that exist among people; in their understanding of the role of culture in people's lives; and in their own knowledge and comfort in working across cultures, particularly as agents of change. New friendships develop over the summer weeks that, for many, evolve into continued relationships and new opportunities when they return home. It is a powerful and life-changing experience.

How can people learn to mediate among those who experience conflict in the world today? What role can young people play in bringing about peace in the world? How might people learn to reach out and touch those from communities that are in conflict? What is the potential for altering one's perception of the enemy? These are critical questions that in many ways underlie a significant amount of intercultural activity today, and adolescents may hold a critical key.

Perhaps more influential than school-based international experiences are those that are possible for young people to participate in during their summer holidays. The Legacy International Youth Program is one such program that provides intensive international and intercultural learning experiences for young people from a variety of backgrounds. Nestled in the foothills of the Blue Ridge Mountains in southern Virginia and founded by the educator, scholar, and humanitarian J. E. Rash, Legacy is a living-learning center devoted to establishing an environment that provides young people with the opportunity to experience life in a global village.

Each summer, up to 200 young people from more than twenty countries leave their homes, some coming from homelands where they endure considerable hostility, to live with peers and learn firsthand about global problems and opportunities, conflict and communication across cultures, leadership in a global context, and social action. Legacy's special talent lies in creating an atmosphere where young people from regions in conflict—from such places as the Middle East, Northern Ireland, Vietnam, Cambodia, and the former Yugoslavia—can come together in a safe space and learn how to see beyond the stereotypes and anxieties they are exposed to at home, ultimately building bonds of friendship and trust that are rather unique among their peers from their region. These young people are actively building bridges where walls typically stand; a sign of hope that things can change and that adversaries from home may be able to shed some of their misunderstandings and begin to trust the "enemy."

It is not easy to establish such a setting, nor is it easy for some of the young people to be in such close contact with one another while they struggle to unlearn many of the hatreds that have become so ingrained at home. It can be equally difficult for others, even young Americans who may come from relatively privileged, peaceful, and secure environments, to witness and participate in the heated dialogues and conversations that take place between conflicting parties. But this is real life, and all become intimately connected with one another throughout the summer as the comfort level and sense of trust grow. All participants must reach beyond their traditional zone of comfort as they learn about others' experiences, develop insight into the global condition, and struggle to understand how each can work to improve upon people's circumstances. One of the long-term goals of Legacy is for young people to become reflective, interculturally sensitive change agents in their communities when they return home—wherever home may be. Thus, in many respects, the entire Legacy experience is an exercise designed to broaden participants' means of perception and thereby prepare young people to function more effectively as global citizens.

Mohammed Darawshe is an Israeli Arab who was affiliated with Legacy from the mid-1980s through the mid-1990s. He was born, and still lives, in the north of Israel—in Iksal, a village that has such a long history that it is mentioned in the New Testament. About 60 percent of the residents of Iksal are related to one another. Iksal is located close to Kibbutz Mizra, a Jewish community founded in 1923 by a group of pioneers from Russia and known worldwide, ironically, for its exceptional sausage products. The city of Afula, an important development town founded in 1925 that serves as the market center of the Jezreel Valley, is nearby. Like most of Israel, this is an extremely culturally diverse region.

Mohammed is an activist who remains committed to establishing linkages between Arabs and Jews, believing that it is only through dialogue, developing mutual understanding, and reconciliation that peace will ever come to this troubled region. He has made this his career, working tirelessly with young people as well as professionals from both sides of the conflict, encouraging them to set aside their differences and learn to listen intently to the pain, struggles, and experiences of the other.

During his time with the summer program, Mohammed is often found sitting with mixed groups, encouraging participants to rethink their present orientation, showing each how his or her present behavior and way of thinking serves to perpetuate problems and the status quo. He does this almost daily; the dialogue at the start of this chapter took place with a group of young people who were preparing to attend a conference in the Mediterranean region later in the summer.

After years of evaluating the summer program in Virginia, Legacy had established a formula that proved quite successful at bringing opposing groups together. Believing they were now ready to try their programs in the "real-world" setting of the Middle East, Legacy organizers sponsored a unique project, the goal of which was to provide a context that would facilitate dialogue and the building of trust among young Israeli Jews, Israeli Arabs, and West Bank Palestinians. The context of an international setting was proposed that would demonstrate to others that it was possible for these parties to come together over a period of time; learn to trust and understand one another; and, ultimately, collaborate in important and very real ways. It was during this particular summer that preparation was under way for this event.

Research on efforts to improve intergroup relations has steadily evolved over the past fifty years (Allport 1954; Sherif 1958; Amir 1969; Stephan 1999; Stephan and Vogt 2004). Central to this research are a number of criteria that appear to be critical when attempting to bring opposing groups together, be they international adversaries or domestic groups in segregated settings. Legacy leaders had, coincidentally, stumbled upon these criteria on their own, and it was reinforcing to find that what they were doing was supported in the research literature on intergroup relations.

Four factors have been identified that facilitate success in improving social contact and intergroup relations and thus reducing prejudice: (1) people should come together to achieve some superordinate goal or common task that could not be achieved without the collaborative efforts of all parties; (2) individuals who come together should have equal status, meaning that they have equal access to any rewards available; (3) administrative support should encourage collaborative efforts; and (4) a high acquaintance potential should exist that encourages rather intimate contact between individuals in a given situation. Incidentally, in addition to being addressed in the summer or other special programs, all of these factors have curricular implications for schools. They can also be integrated and applied in well-developed travel programs.

Superordinate Goals. Individuals who come together and work toward achieving some superordinate goal or common task that could not be satisfied without the participation of all involved are more likely to learn to get along. This concept stems from the work of Sherif (1958), who worked, like Legacy, among children in summer camps. Sherif found that it was relatively easy to create hostility and aggression between two groups of boys at summer camp, to the point that name calling, food fights, and cabin raids at night were common. He found it quite difficult, however, to bring these groups of children back together again as one larger, cooperative group. Finally, after much trial and error, camp staff staged an incident in which a bus got stuck in the mud while on the way to an outing. In order for the bus to continue on its way, all of the campers had to work together to push the bus back onto the road. This superordinate goal, which could not have been achieved without everyone's participation, provided the means to bring the two opposing groups together.

In the school context, teachers can apply this criterion in any number of ways. Superordinate goals are readily available in the form of team sports, drama productions, and music performances, as well as through cooperative learning activities that can be easily integrated into the classroom setting. In the Legacy summer camp experience, numerous opportunities are present that encourage groups of young people, many who originate in countries in conflict, to come together to achieve some superordinate task. In addition to the everyday needs of maintaining a certain degree of cleanliness and orderliness at camp, programming requires these young people to collaborate in the preparation and presentation of a number of cultural programs depicting the people from their region of the world. Thus, Irish Catholics and Protestants come together to make a presentation on Ireland and Irish culture; or Israeli Jews and Arabs come together with the task of presenting a balanced view of their part of the world.

Although it is never easy, over the weeks these young people inevitably work through their differences as well as their apprehensions and develop a level of trust and friendship among one another that could not have been achieved in their homeland. In the process they also learn a significant amount about each other's culture, their particular circumstances, and the chance for peace and reconciliation.

Equal-Status Contact. Working in integrated school settings in Israel, Amir (1969) found that if individuals coming together perceive that they have equal status, or equal access to any rewards available, conditions are set for improved relations. Travelers who look closely at the social fabric in many countries find that although they are given equal status on paper, many citizens may not, in reality, have all the benefits afforded others in that particular nation. This was certainly evident under segregation in the American South until the civil rights movement took hold in the 1960s, under apartheid in South Africa until the early 1990s, or in some countries of the Middle East.

Visitors to Switzerland, on the other hand, quickly learn that French, German, and Italian are all recognized as official languages of the country, with official documents and most communication to the public made available in all three languages. Or in Canada, French and English are both recognized as official languages. In these nations, speakers of diverse languages, and thus cultural backgrounds, are all appreciated, well informed, and encouraged to participate in the society at large. Such a practice seems quite different in comparison to the United States, where the current movement in many states is to make English the official language—even though the United States boasts the fourth- or fifth-largest Spanish-speaking population in the world. It is important that students understand and experience how other societies successfully integrate their diverse constituencies, and travel is one way to point this out.

In the summer camp setting of Legacy, young people share cabins as well as daily chores with others from around the world. Legacy works hard to bring an equalizing force to all of the participants, believing that not only should the young people from overseas experience culture shock, but the American participants should as well. Thus, all participants are provided a vegetarian, natural foods diet—something to which all have to stretch and adjust. It is a leveling experience, providing all with something to learn and experience together. And through the reduction of the sugars and dyes in many foods, young people's energy level changes dramatically, and they are better able to engage in long dialogue with one another about some very sensitive topics.

On a global scale, the environment is perhaps the most visible or tangible evidence we have that demonstrates how all forms of life are interconnected. It was with this in mind that Legacy, very wisely, chose the environmental condition of the Mediterranean Sea as a common theme to explore for its summer conference; a superordinate task, so to speak—something that could bring Arabs and Jews, as well as others in the region, together.

But bringing Arabs and Jews together for such a program had never before been successfully achieved. Here is where the subtlety and power of the summer program came into play, and how it served as an orientation and preparation for something greater. Legacy developed a plan to invite four youth leaders between the ages of sixteen and twenty-one from most of the nations that border the Mediterranean to an environmental conference in Cartagena, Spain. That is, four young people from such countries as France, Spain, Italy, Greece, Turkey, Lebanon, Israel, Morocco, Egypt, the United States, Israel, and Jordan, were to be nominated by an environmental agency in their nation to participate in the conference, to learn about the broader region, and to consider long-term, joint activities.

A message often promoted by Legacy is, "What appears to be primary may actually be secondary, and what appears to be secondary may actually be primary." Thus, while on the surface this conference would appear to be of environmental concern, and in fact that was its emphasis, the primary purpose of the effort that was at work behind the scenes was to create a venue that brought Arabs and Jews together in a collaborative, equal-status project. What appeared to be primary, the environmental conference, actually was secondary; and what appeared to be secondary, the bringing together of people from different backgrounds, actually was the primary purpose of the event.

In the school context, equal access to rewards can mean that all students have equal access to knowledge as well as extracurricular offerings. Teachers who are knowledgeable about the impact of culture on learning style and other behavior are more inclined to employ culturally relevant curricula and instructional strategies in the classroom, thus ensuring that more students achieve. Of equal importance is the necessity to encourage all students to participate in extracurricular activities in school—which may include travel. But because of the inequities in the socioeconomic status among many children in schools, those from lower socioeconomic groups may never have the opportunity to participate in after-school activities, let alone travel programs. Thus, they do not gain the benefits these offerings provide.

Administrative Support. In order to be effective, efforts to reduce prejudice and improve intergroup relations must be seen as important at all levels of an organization. Such efforts cannot be seen entirely as the whim or "cause" of a particular group or individual. In the context of the Legacy summer program, counselors and administrators always focus their attention on dialogue and making evident to all how people should come together to discuss their differences. In the school context, teachers and school administrators must actively encourage and show support for such efforts.

High Acquaintance Potential. A fourth tenet from the intergroup relations literature is that people should come together in such a way that they have intimate, close contact with one another. In this way, people get to know one another beyond the stereotypes that generally prevail.

It was obvious how this was attained during the summer program, where participants shared common living quarters, meals, recreational time, and so forth. To guarantee success at the conference in Spain, Legacy planned to "seed" the project by introducing a significant number of participants to one another before the larger gathering took place. Thus, ten American alumni from the summer program would travel to both Egypt and Israel prior to the conference to serve as bridge builders. In Egypt, they would join a group of ten Egyptian young people and would spend a week in Cairo and the Sinai studying Egyptian culture and learning about the local environment while simultaneously bonding as a group. Representatives from the Egyptian contingent would be invited to the conference that was to occur two weeks later. From Egypt, the group of Americans would travel to Israel and join a group of ten Israeli Jewish and ten Israeli Arab young people from various communities in Israel and the West Bank. Together, this group would study one another's cultures and learn about the environment of the region. Then, representatives from this group who had already developed a comfort level would travel to the conference site in Spain, where they would join representatives from the other participating nations.

It was in Israel a few weeks before the conference that the American team from Legacy, a group that included Stephan and Sarah, was reunited with Rema, Ibrahim, and Schmuel, along with a few others who had attended Legacy in previous summers. This group was warm and welcoming from the outset, and the new Jewish and Arab participants from the region who joined them found it easy to fit in. The group in Israel now numbered about thirty.

In Israel, while actively studying the local environment of the Negev, the young people were also engaged in a number of cultural encounters designed to enhance everyone's understanding of Arab and Jewish culture as well as the conflicts inherent in the region. The program was to include visits to Arab villages and Jewish communities, as well as an experience in Jerusalem. An underlying objective was for the American participants to serve as a bridge and assist these Jewish and Arab young people to get to know one another beyond the stereotypes that were rampant in their lives. For the most part, as Rema had hinted back at Legacy, Arab and Jewish communities remain rather isolated from one another; interaction is restricted to brief encounters in the marketplace or perhaps in another work setting. Children in both communities, even though they are in close proximity, grow up having limited, if any, contact with one another. Thus they gain little substantial firsthand information about the other, and the stereotypes and anxieties they learn in their respective communities are perpetuated.

After the first week of environmental education in Israel, and once a certain level of trust and friendship had been established, the program turned its focus to that of culture and the cross-cultural experience. The goal of this effort was to get to a point where the young people could spend a couple of nights with families in one another's communities; that is, Jewish young people would spend a few nights in an Arab village, and Arab youth would spend the same amount of time with Jewish families. Suddenly those enjoyable and friendly times spent outdoors and in various activities with "the other" became extremely stressful as each participant began thinking about what it would be like to live in the other's homes. Some had visions of being kidnapped in the night, or being beaten or robbed by others in the community; that's how strong the stereotypes and fear of the other had become. Anxiety aside, the young people each went off to their respective host families with their characteristic openness and trust.

After the homestay experience, the participants came together to share their experiences. Schmuel was among the first to discuss his feelings about the homestay during a debriefing session.

"I really wasn't too concerned about staying in the village when we had planned this portion of the trip," he said. "After all, during the summer I had become rather close to Rema and a few of the other participants. I trusted her and truly believed she was a friend. But when we got to the village I suddenly realized that this was not Rema's home. No one there knew anything about me and I would have to begin at step one in establishing a relationship.

"The family was welcoming to me, and the food was fabulous. I was surprised that I found quite a few similarities between our two cultures. What shocked me, though, was how anxious and nervous I became, and to be honest, I had trouble sleeping the first night. The sounds outside my window were different, some of the smells in the house were not familiar, and I was not quite sure what would happen in the morning. I was pleasantly surprised when I woke up. Many from the extended family were coming in and out of the house all morning long, I think, in part, to interact with me as I was a bit of an oddity. I was a bit nervous and unsure throughout most of the morning. And to be honest, I was really looking forward to when we would all get together that afternoon. But it all went well. And I really enjoyed the wedding celebration we were able to observe the final night in the village."

J. E. Rash, founder of Legacy and program director for much of the Israel experience, spoke next. "What kinds of conversations did you have with members of the families or others in the communities? And what did you learn from them?"

Ibrahim reflected calmly, "It was awkward at first. We talked about lots of surface things—similarities in food and language, for instance, just like Schmuel said."

"We typically refer to that as surface level or objective culture," offered Rash, listening intently. "Objective culture refers to those aspects of a people that are visible or tangible, things that all can see and discuss rather easily. The more powerful aspects of culture, though, are its hidden, more subjective elements, sometimes referred to as deep culture. Here we are talking about such things as people's values, attitudes, and the way they interact with one another. These are much more difficult to get out on the table and discuss. But they are a critical dimension of all people and their interactions."

"Well," Ibrahim continued, "we eventually began to talk about the current conflict. But I had to bring it up. Up until that time we were all being polite to one another. I asked the father what he felt about the current situation."

"And what did he say?" asked Rash.

"He felt that we are all suffering under the current circumstances, and he blamed the leaders on both sides. He believed that most of the people really want peace and that they were willing to negotiate a just settlement. He was very concerned about the recent increase in what he called terrorist attacks. I tried to help him see that my people consider what the Israelis are doing as terrorist activities. He couldn't see that, however. But he was obviously interested and willing to talk with us. He truly wanted to learn about my family and how we are coping with the situation. I felt good about that. I guess it was a beginning."

Schmuel spoke up again. "I learned quite a lot from my host family. I have never really spent a long time with an Arab family. They, too, were very hospitable. I'd say everything I'd ever heard about Arab hospitality was true, and after a while I felt quite comfortable. I was uncomfortable bringing up the topic of the conflict, but the father and his brothers were not. They didn't seem angry at me, but they did speak quite heatedly about the situation. This is really the first time I had ever spoken face to face with Palestinian families that were affected by the situation. They told me that their family village was destroyed after the war in 1948. Some of their family had moved to Jordan, some were killed in the conflict, and others remained in Israel. It's been very difficult for them to remain together and keep in touch, and they really feel displaced by all the problems. They did say that they understood the need for a Jewish state, especially after the Holocaust. But they also insisted that all the people in Israel could live together, side by side, and that perhaps we all had an obligation to learn to do this as a model for the rest of the world. I was quite taken by that thought. I'd never really thought Arabs could feel that way."

Then Rema spoke. "I had similar feelings when we stayed with the Jewish families. It took a while, but I was finally able to relax and feel comfortable. The kids in the family were nice enough, but you could tell that they, too, were unsure of things and how the few days would be. I'm glad I had the opportunity to stay with them. We talked a bit about the conflict. The younger kids in the family, once they spoke up, began to blame me for the current situation. I guess I can understand that from the perspective of a young child; if there was any blame to give, it would be targeted at me as I was a Palestinian in their community and seen as the enemy. The parents, however, quickly jumped into the conversation and helped their children see things from another point of view."

J. E. Rash posed one final question, this one particularly for the Americans to consider.

"I want you all to think about your role in perpetuating or resolving this conflict—especially the Americans. What will *you* do once you return home?"

It was on Thursday, around lunchtime, that the group traveled on toward Jerusalem. It was here that they would spend the last three days in Israel before departing for the conference in Spain. There was a sense of anticipation among all. For both the Jewish and Arab participants, Jerusalem represents one of the most important sites for both Judaism and Islam. For the Americans, both Jewish and Gentile, it was their first experience in this city that reflects so much controversy.

Jerusalem may be the holiest city in the world, considering the number and diversity of people who refer to it as their sacred place. For Jews it is the site of Solomon's Temple, the City of David, and capital of the Israelite nation. For Christians it is where Jesus spent the last days of his ministry and where the Last Supper, the Crucifixion, and the Resurrection took place. And for Muslims, Jerusalem is where the prophet Muhammad ascended to heaven. Although it is visited by thousands of pilgrims and sages each year from all three of these major religions, it has experienced thirty centuries of struggle and strife. While it is a place of beauty and divinity, it is also a place of mystery and paradox—and a city of contradictions. Referred to by many, ironically, as the City of Peace, Jerusalem has a history of conflict that rivals most any place in the world, crying out during its troubled history.

I had visited Jerusalem a few times prior to this visit, but not with all the tensions and concerns of the moment, there having been a major confrontation in the West Bank just two days earlier. And never had I been in the city with a mixed group of Arabs and Jews. There was a silence on the bus as we drove along the highway from Tel Aviv and passed, on both sides of the road, the remains of military vehicles and monuments to fallen soldiers, which repeatedly reminded us of the struggles and the Jewish lives that had been lost. I wondered how our Arab participants felt as we made our way toward the city. One passes no such reminders of Arab losses, and there are no memorials along the road when one enters Jerusalem from other directions.

Looking out over the city from the Mount of Olives is an awe-inspiring sight: from this vantage point one can see directly to the Old City, the Dome of the Rock glistening brightly in the sunlight. After posing for a number of photos with Jerusalem at our backs, the group drove down toward the Old City. Upon entering the Old City, one immediately senses the tensions as well as the possibilities that permeate the entire region. Old Jerusalem is divided into four quarters—an Armenian sector, a Christian sector, a Muslim sector, and a Jewish sector. One can find almost anything, from the freshest of foods and spices, to leather goods, musical instruments, fine clothes, and jewelry, among the hundreds of shops that line the narrow streets. Shopkeepers and shoppers alike banter back and forth as they seek to agree upon a fair price for the goods and services available. Meandering among these close quarters, one is just as likely to rub elbows with an Orthodox Jewish seminary student, a devout Muslim cleric, a religious Christian on a pilgrimage, or young students from all walks of life wearing their uniform of a T-shirt and jeans.

The Dung Gate, one of the seven entry points to the Old City, so called because it is from here that garbage was removed from the city in earlier times, opens to the Jewish Quarter. Entering amid tight security, one can't help but take notice of the Western Wall. Located in the midst of the Jewish Quarter, this is the section of the western supporting wall of the Temple Mount that has remained intact since the destruction of the Second Temple in 70 C.E. Since about 1520, all literary sources describe it as a place of assembly and prayer for Jews. Thus, it has become the most sacred spot in Jewish consciousness and tradition, being a center of mourning over the destruction of the Temple. Since then it has been known as the Wailing Wall. From 1948 until 1967, Jews had no access to this area. After Jews regained control of the Old City, the area in front of the Western Wall was cleared and converted into a large paved open space. The lower square near the Wall is an area set aside for prayer where one finds Jews praying or studying, either singly or in groups, both day and night. Hands that have touched the wall in prayer throughout the centuries seem to have polished the surface of the stone. Today it is even possible to fax your prayer to individuals and groups who will insert it in the wall. Thus, prayers from around the world find their way to the wall each and every day in a kind of technology-to-theology connection.

Just over the Western Wall lies the Dome of the Rock with its golden dome that can be seen lighting up the Old City from most anywhere. The Tenth Caliph, Abd al-Malik ibn Marwan, built the great Dome of the Rock between 687 and 691 as a shrine for pilgrims. Perhaps the greatest monumental building in early Islamic history, it stands twenty meters high and ten meters in diameter. This reportedly is the spot from which Muhammad ascended to heaven. The dome was originally covered in pure gold, and today its anodized aluminum skin is seen from miles around. Adjacent to the Dome is the Al-Aqsa Mosque.

As we arrived at the Wailing Wall, both men and women, separated from one another, were worshipping. A few of our participants, Stephan among them, approached the wall to offer prayers. A few tourists could be seen having their Bar Mitzvahs at this sacred site. We could hear the afternoon call to prayer coming from over the wall, and a few of the Muslim members of our group went to pray. At the time of this visit one could still move freely between the sites. It is, unfortunately, forbidden today.

The spiritual energy of this region has been enriched by the many different groups that have laid claim to the city over the centuries, as well as by the many individuals who continue to be drawn to it. By all means, this is a sacred site that radiates a force that no modern spiritual seeker should miss.

All the young people were moved by the experience of the afternoon, and this served as a backdrop for the last two days in Israel. The spiritual underpinnings, although discussed only briefly, seemed to permeate the group as the participants prepared for travel to the conference site in Spain. There was much discussion among the Israelis and Palestinians in the group about what they would do when they returned from the conference.

Rema began. "When I stayed with the Jewish family, we talked about the possibility of meeting once we returned from the conference. I think my parents would even be interested in the possibility of meeting with the family. And the children and I talked about the possibility of getting our schools to do some joint activity."

"And Ibrahim and I talked about doing something similar when we get back," added Schmuel. "Once he gets his driver's license and saves some money from working, we're going to visit one another. I'm excited about that possibility. In our own reality at home, this would never seem possible. Now that we've had these summer experiences, I think other things might be promising."

Sarah finally spoke up. "I guess this has been a real dose of reality for me. I continually have to challenge the stereotypes I grew up with, and I guess that's a good thing. But it sure is difficult, not really having much of a background in these affairs. This experience has opened my eyes up to so much, and I'm glad I had a chance to participate in it. I feel emotionally exhausted, but refreshed and enriched nonetheless. I hope I have the energy to sustain myself during the conference in Spain."

While we should not be naive about the tensions that have continued to exist in the years since these early meetings occurred, there still are signs of hope. It is very satisfying to turn on CNN, for instance, and see some of these former participants being interviewed and still expressing optimism and hope that things can improve. Many of these young people, now young adults, continue to work toward reconciliation and understanding. This, alone, is an important lesson for us all.

8

THE MAKING OF WORLD-CLASS TEACHERS: INTERNATIONAL STUDENT TEACHING

Now I realize that the United States is not the center of the universe.

—American student teacher abroad

The room was alive with excited chatter when I entered. This is typical, and exactly what I expect to see whenever students get together upon returning from their overseas student teaching. Many unexpectedly find themselves feeling rather alone and unique among their peers, having few with whom to share their experience. This is unfortunate, as sharing and processing an influential international experience is vital if one is to truly integrate what he or she has experienced. Many in the group were busy sharing their photo albums and relating stories of their experiences. Lakesha and Anita were especially animated, relating stories of similar places they had visited and people they had met while in Australia, both having taught in the same school in a suburb of Melbourne only two years apart. It was difficult for me to settle the group down and to focus a discussion.

Most American teachers and teacher-education students are relatively inexperienced when it comes to intercultural affairs, and the demographics of the profession don't leave us with much hope that things will be much different in the near future (Zimpher 1989; Cushner, McClelland,

and Safford 2003). American teachers tend to be a relatively homogeneous group, nearly 90 percent European American and middle class, and approximately two-thirds female. They are, by and large, cross-culturally inexperienced and have limited knowledge and experience living or working with other cultures. Close to 70 percent of white teacher-education students reportedly spend all or most of their free time with people of their own racial or ethnic background. The majority have limited expectations for the success of all learners and believe that low-income and minority students are not capable of learning higher-level concepts in the subjects they are preparing to teach. Teachers also tend to be linguistically limited, with fewer than 10 percent claiming fluency in any second language and fully three-fifths being monolingual.

Teachers are also rather narrowly focused and have quite limited horizons when it comes to their international aspirations. The majority of teacher candidates live within one hundred miles of where they were born, and most wish to teach where they grew up or in areas very similar to where they are from. And, of all college majors, teacher-education students have the least knowledge of and interest in international affairs.

While there may not be much optimism in this information, those who embark on an international student-teaching venture are taking the first steps toward changing this reality. They are fast becoming "world-class teachers," as they immerse themselves in a new culture and struggle to adjust, not only interpersonally, but professionally as well. And this is no easy task.

The Consortium for Overseas Student Teaching (COST) has been placing student teachers overseas since 1972. Since its inception, hundreds of American students have had the opportunity to teach in national schools in such countries as England, Scotland, Ireland, Wales, Australia, New Zealand, South Africa, Canada, and the Bahamas, as well as in international English-speaking schools in Switzerland, Greece, Italy, Japan, Mexico, Ecuador, and Costa Rica. While most of these destinations represent relatively easy places for student teachers to adjust to, and their teaching is always in English, for most of these students, teaching abroad for eight to fifteen weeks is a life-changing experience (Cushner and Mahon 2002; Mahon and Cushner 2002).

Reunions of students who have completed their student teaching overseas are common among COST sending institutions. It was in such

THE MAKING OF WORLD-CLASS TEACHERS

a setting that Lakesha and Anita, introduced at the beginning of the chapter, met. In total, six students who had spent between eight and twelve weeks completing their student teaching in an overseas setting came together for an afternoon debriefing session: Megan, a twenty-two-year-old European American who had just returned from teaching in a primary school in Ireland; Anita, a European American, now twenty-five, who had taught sixth grade in Australia two years earlier; Tom, a twenty-two-year-old European American math teacher who had completed his teaching in a secondary school in New Zealand one year earlier and who had returned to teach there for one year; Lakesha, an African American who, at the age of twenty-two, had gone to Australia to teach upper elementary language arts; Keenan, a quiet and reserved thirty-eight-year-old African American man who, having embarked upon a second career, was our first student to go to South Africa to teach upper elementary grades; and Donna, a twenty-one-year-old European American who had recently returned from Mexico.

Once the group had settled down, I began. "Much of the research says that people develop increased self-confidence and independence as a result of an international experience. People are said to become more tolerant and adaptable in their approach to life. In other words, there is a lot of personal development that occurs as a result of an international experience. Would you agree with this?"

"For me, this was really the first time I was totally on my own and had to rely solely on myself," offered Donna. "I was confronted with many new and different situations, some that even scared me at times and some I did not totally agree with. Yet, I had to act and make the right decision if I was to be successful. This was also the first time I had to navigate around a large city, and Mexico City is the largest city in the world, approaching something around 20 million people. Now *that* made me a bit nervous—I come from a small town of about 25,000 people. But I made it, and I survived! And now I think I can do just about anything."

"I was the only African American in my school and community," added Lakesha. "At first I was scared and a bit nervous about going to Australia. Many people asked me why, as an African American, I would want to go there. I had read about the struggles of the Aborigines. I was interested in their experience and in learning about their culture, but at the same time I was a bit nervous that I might suffer some of the same discrimination they had encountered. I didn't find this to be the case at all. Most people were really welcoming and interested in me as a person as well as in my African American heritage. Many doors opened up for me, both in the school and in the community, especially through my host family. While it may have been stressful at the beginning, I found I was able to adapt in this environment. Now I know that, as a result of this experience, I can do just about anything I put my mind to. I've become much more independent and self-sufficient than I ever thought I could become. And I've learned to take chances in my life, something that I really never did before. I've also learned a lot about a couple of other cultures, both Australian Aborigines and white Australians, and for that I'm really grateful."

"Traveling to a world unknown was quite a brave step for me," said Anita. "I didn't realize exactly how brave I was until I got there. There were many 'unknowns' in my experience, even in Australia, another English-speaking country. Prior to my Australian experience, many little inconveniences would cause me to go into a panic. That's not so now. While I was in Australia, there was a huge gas explosion in our neighborhood. We were out of hot water for almost two weeks. Trust me, nothing shakes me now."

"I remember hearing about that incident," Lakesha responded. "They're still talking about how that experience brought the community together and how many new friendships developed."

"Being totally responsible for finding a place to live in a large foreign city was one of the most difficult things about my experience," added Tom. "At first I thought it strange that no one had arranged any housing for me. But my supervisor said that he couldn't predict the kind of living arrangement I would like, so he asked me to find my own housing. I guess it saves problems for him later if people are unhappy with a host family or an apartment he chose. It took me a few days, but eventually I found a room to rent that was close to the school. And I met some pretty nice people as a result of this that I got together with on a regular basis. The experience made me more independent, and I feel that I can do anything now. In fact, I was offered a teaching position in maths—that's how they refer to math in New Zealand—at the school in which I student taught. I came home in December after finishing my student teaching, graduated, visited family and friends, and four weeks later turned around and went back for another year. That's been the best year of my life. Now I know that I can make it through anything no matter what it is."

There was a pause in the conversation as Tom went over and helped himself to a cup of coffee.

"Many people return from an overseas experience and say their perceptions have changed. Did any of you experience this, and, if so, in what ways?" I asked.

Lakesha began. "I was excited about my first overseas experience and was glad to be able to teach at the same time. But it was quite overwhelming, and I was a bit stressed at the beginning. It was difficult trying to learn another culture, to fit into another school, and to learn their national curriculum all at the same time. I just took it one step at a time and I did it! At first, I thought I had a lot to share with the Australians; and perhaps I did. But they had so much more to give to me. I know I was told about this during my orientation; that I shouldn't just barge right in with all that I know but should take some time to learn from others. But this still caught me by surprise. I always thought that everyone wanted to learn from America; that everyone wanted to be American. And even though Australians really seemed to look to us in so many ways, I now know that the United States is not the center of the universe. Australians know so much more about the United States than I knew about them, and I think that's a shame."

"That is similar to what I found when I was in Australia," added Anita. "I was rather embarrassed at first, especially about how little I seemed to know, both about them as well as about most of the rest of the world. But the Australians seemed to take it in stride, after they poked a bit of fun at me. It was almost as if they expected me to be that way. I often wondered why it was that Australians expected me to be somewhat naive about the rest of the world. Now I know. They were right about a lot of things. Americans in general, and many of the teachers I now teach with, know relatively little about the rest of the world. I think that is a shame." Others were nodding their heads in agreement but remained silent.

"What about some of the others of you? What stands out from your experience that you'd like to share? What are some things you experienced, and how might this impact your teaching?" I asked.

"I had to get over my fear of sounding stupid using the Spanish language when I first arrived in Mexico," Donna offered. "Although I'd studied Spanish in high school I really couldn't speak it to anyone else. But using it daily with my host family and with the kids in the school, even though they all spoke English, was the only way that I was ever going to be able to speak the language. But now, I can be more understanding of people from elsewhere who come to America and have to learn English. It is very difficult when you are older and can be depressing and scary when you can't communicate what you want to be known."

"I also experienced issues related to language and thought about how linguistically limited we are in the United States," Megan interjected. "After I taught in Ireland I traveled quite a bit around the European continent. In the United States, you can travel thousands of miles and rarely hear another language. In Europe, it's much different. I guess in Europe, and many other places in the world for that matter, one would be surrounded with different languages growing up as a child. I think we're at a disadvantage when it comes to this.

"I also learned how to empathize with others, and to be sensitive to the needs of children at a much higher level," Megan continued. "Being in a new and different situation gave me the opportunity to experience what it feels like to be away from one's familiar surroundings and to be the odd person out. It can be very scary and lonely at times, but you do get over it. This is one way I have become more sensitive. This will definitely help me if I ever get a student who is from another country, or even another state, in my classroom. I learned so much, especially about myself. I also learned that teaching is a passion of mine that I cannot wait to pursue."

"I had a similar experience," added Tom. "In New Zealand, I learned what it was like to be an outsider, to not understand what others around me take for granted. This is extremely helpful to me as I think about teaching children from different backgrounds now that I am back home. I learned how to be accepting of differences. Even people completely different from you have something in common. I learned to listen to what others are interested in and what they believe. I also learned to be much less suspicious of people and to trust people much more than I ever had before. I met some incredibly nice, giving people. Most of the time, people are good and can be much more helpful and kind than I had ever thought."

Donna spoke next. "I can use my experiences to help introduce my students to the differences and cultural experiences our world is made up of. I can teach understanding of these differences since I have become aware of them on a firsthand basis. I will also be more aware of the differences that each student may have from one another and help these students adapt to new and possibly difficult situations. And although I never really particularly cared for social studies, now I think it's one of the most important subjects I can teach my students. And I can do it in so many ways that go beyond the textbook. I attribute this to my overseas experience."

A silence fell upon the group once again.

"Keenan, you've been rather quiet through this discussion. What was your experience like in South Africa?" I asked. "I imagine it was quite different from many of the others."

"Well, in some ways it was, but in other ways it was similar. I became more independent as the others did, that's for sure. I had a wonderful experience, but I was very lonely and I had a difficult adjustment in the beginning. My host family was wonderful, though. I stayed with one of the teachers from the school I taught at in Port Elizabeth. He was very helpful and gracious to me. But when I went out into the community; now that was a different story. It's a pretty stressful life in South Africa right now as they go about the transition from apartheid to a free and democratic society. Both whites and blacks are undergoing a change, and it's not been easy for either side. And the economic situation in the country is quite different from anything I have ever experienced. So many people are out of work and have little hope for their future. Yet there is an optimism among many that things will improve. After all, most of the world thought South Africa would explode in a civil war during the election when Nelson Mandela stepped down. But that didn't happen. That was a positive sign for the rest of the world, I think. The people are hopeful and they have so much to overcome. I was glad to be a small part of that effort."

Keenan stopped to catch his breath.

"Did you feel prepared for your experience?" asked Megan.

"That's a hard one," Keenan replied. "I was prepared for certain things. I knew about culture shock, for instance, and I remember thinking that it wouldn't happen to me. But it did—on many occasions. I think I kind of naively thought that because I was black that my visit to

Africa would be easy. But there were many times when I just didn't understand what was going on. When that happened, I remembered some of the things that we had talked about in our orientation sessions. You know, about the adjustment cycle and things like that, so I knew I wasn't alone in my feelings. But I wasn't prepared for the racial tensions that existed. And I'm not sure there is any way I could have been prepared for them, as racial issues there are so much different than they are in the United States. I read a bit about the situation before I left, so I knew a few of the current issues. But until you really begin to meet people and learn about their experience firsthand, it is hard to understand the situation. That is why I'm now a firm believer in the educational value of travel. Now I can begin to understand the plight of others around the world because I have experienced it myself. This is so much better than reading about it in a book or in the newspaper. I think more teachers should have such experiences; it would make school a much more real and alive place. I hope to be able to offer similar experiences, although probably on a smaller scale, to my students once I begin teaching."

"What do you know about the process of culture learning now that you've all had an overseas experience?" I asked.

"Once I was out of the United States," Lakesha replied, "I was able to turn around, in effect, and look back upon my own country and view it from a different perspective. And you know, I didn't always like what I saw. For instance, I learned that other countries are not as openly racist as in the United States, and that other cultures seem to be more open to minorities. I felt more welcome as an African American in Australia than I typically do at home."

Anita entered the conversation. "Apart from learning to better deal with stressful situations, I also was put in a position where I had to evaluate my own cultural beliefs. Before this trip, I knew no other culture than my own. Why does my country celebrate Halloween—a commemoration of evil spirits? Why do so many people in other countries think that Americans all run around with guns? These were questions I was forced to answer."

Donna was next to respond. "To help people adjust and learn, they should allow themselves to live the way that specific culture lives. They should involve themselves in the traditions, the government, and way things are done locally. At first it seems so foreign and you just want things to be the way you've always known them to be. Open up your mind and think like the people who surround you."

"I'd say the same thing," added Tom. "Become involved in the local community when possible. If environmental issues concern them, as they so often do in New Zealand, concern yourself. Or if cultural issues are a focus, learn about them, attend community meetings, and try to identify with local needs. There was much concern among the Maori people in our community that their children's needs were not being met in school. It took me a while, but eventually I learned quite a bit about Maori culture and the current situation. I even learned to speak a little Maori language as a way to understand the people more. And this proved to be extremely useful in helping me meet people and reach some of the parents in the school community. The more you involve yourself the more you will learn, but you have to realize that it takes time. I was just beginning to really understand things when I finished my student teaching. It was only really when I returned that I could integrate more fully in the community. Understanding another culture takes a considerable amount of time."

Megan chimed in, "Because my mind has been opened to other worlds, I think differently than those who have not experienced other cultures. I have become much more multicultural in my view of the world. I now believe that multicultural education happens every day, and that this can become a mind-set for the teacher—rather than an occasional effort. It is something that has changed my life and I will never be the same. I owe this to my overseas teaching experience."

I posed one final question to the group. "Is there anything that I've not asked you that you'd like to share or discuss with the group?"

"Well," said Tom, "to be honest, and I don't really know how to say this, but when I first got back to the United States I remember thinking how fat everyone looked. Americans, in general, just appear to be much more overweight than did the New Zealanders."

There was laughter around the room.

"I felt the same thing," added Megan. "I spent the first few days just observing people. But then I considered that I was now beginning to observe my own culture, and I was learning some significant things, not all of which I liked. I thought of people as overweight, superficial, lazy, and loud. Everyone seemed *so* loud!"

"After the experience I had of not having hot water for two weeks, I began to questions all the material things we depend upon back home," added Anita. "It really was no big deal if we couldn't wash our clothes when and where we wanted; we just went to a Laundromat in the next town one day. And I managed to take cold showers; it wasn't that bad! We have so many conveniences that we take for granted at home that many people around the world just don't have. We really can live without a lot of the conveniences we think we need. I know I've become less materialistic as a result of this experience."

"I agree with you, Anita," Donna chimed in. "The students I worked with, both in the school as well as the college students I met while in Mexico, didn't have all the computer accessibility that we now take for granted; they just shared so much more, or did without. We have so much here that we really can get along without if we had to. Sometimes it's embarrassing when I compare my life to others."

"I often had to defend American policies and actions while I was away," said Keenan. "While the blacks in South Africa were pleased that the United States participated in the boycott of the country during apartheid, certainly not all of the whites were. And now, there is considerable criticism of how the United States seems to impose itself in many countries overseas. There was lots of controversy over the price of prescriptive medications to fight AIDS while I was in South Africa, for instance. The whole world says it's concerned about the high incidence of AIDS in southern Africa, but the drug companies fought really hard to keep the prices so high that few Africans could afford them. While I didn't necessarily agree with these practices, I had to explain and sometimes defend them.

"America's poor record of involvement in the Palestinian–Israeli issue was a special concern to many people, as were our actions in Iraq and elsewhere. And here, again, I had to explain our policies and actions, even if I didn't agree with them. It was hard at times, and I wasn't really prepared to do this. But whenever anything big happened in the world, people would come right over to me and ask for my insights. I couldn't always give them an answer they were satisfied with. I'd suggest that other people planning to live overseas become more knowledgeable about world affairs as well as what's going on within our own country. Read the *New York Times* or *Newsweek* magazine for weeks before you leave so you can speak, rather intelligently, about things going on in the world."

"So it sounds as if some of you may have also become more knowledgeable about U.S. policies and practices, or at least the perception of them, from another perspective," I said. "You've also become more critical and perhaps more reflective of your own culture. I wonder how this might impact your teaching in the future. How many of you will encourage your students to become more analytical, more reflective, more critical because now you, yourself, have these skills. It may take some time until we find this out."

While it may not be possible to generalize from any one student or any one statement, there is the sense that a significant amount of learning does occur for these student teachers and that this can impact their behavior when they are teaching back home. This learning, it should be pointed out, is generally nonformal or nonacademic in nature. That is, these student teachers have been active participants in the lives of students and teachers in schools in other countries and, as a result, have learned a significant amount that could not be taught in any textbook or by any lecture. This is consistent with what experiential learning theorists have known about learning in general for years, and what cross-cultural psychologists and intercultural trainers have known about the process of culture learning. The lived experience allows individuals to become fully engaged over an extended period of time, which is critical to the learning process. Starting from the concrete experience, people can then begin to reflect upon their observations, consider them abstractly, and form generalizations, and they can subsequently test the viability of those concepts back in real-life settings. And now these internationally experienced student teachers become internationally oriented teachers in their own classrooms, passing this orientation on to the students in their charge.

9

BEYOND TOURISM: THE IMPORTANCE OF EXPERIENCE ON IMPACT

> Keep your hands open, and all the sands of the desert can pass through them. Close them, and all you can feel is a bit of grit.
>
> —T. Deshimaru

"I'll bet you don't recognize me," the bartender said with a slight smirk as he handed me my drink, "but I know you."

My curiosity was piqued. I had stopped at a local bar to meet a few colleagues before we all headed off to a university function. I studied the face of this young man who appeared to be in his late twenties. He could have been a former student of mine, and I'm usually good at remembering faces. But a lot of changes can occur in twenty years.

My friends stared in my direction, wondering how I would respond.

"Gee, I'm afraid I just don't recognize you," I said, somewhat embarrassed. "Were you a student of mine at the university school?"

"Now you're getting close. I will say that I think it is because of you and the trip we took to Belize when I was ten years old that I am the kind of person I am today. We had such an incredible experience there. And you really did a fine job of taking what could have been a two-week trip and turning it into an experience that lasted the year for the class, and then a lifetime for me. I remember that when I first came back from

Belize, I felt quite different from those who did not go with us. And it took me a while to understand this and the impact that the experience had on me. But I can tell you that, even though the trip was not necessarily easy, I am not a prejudiced person as are so many others I went to high school with. And I want to thank you for that."

My colleagues were suitably impressed. Now where was the promotion and tenure committee when I needed it? Teachers seldom have the privilege of knowing the impact of their work, as it is the rare student who comes forward with thanks and appreciation for the influence they had on his or her development. This was proof enough for me that something quite influential had gone on in the lives of these young students many years earlier. Thank you, Tom, for coming forward and sharing your experience with me, and with my colleagues.

THE IMPACT OF LIVING AND STUDYING ABROAD

What actually happens as a result of an overseas experience? What changes are evident in people's lives; in their thinking, their attitudes, and their behavior? What occurs educationally that accounts for these changes? This chapter looks at the impact of the international experience and the role of experience in the attainment of new knowledge and skill.

There have been increasing efforts over the years to understand the impact that an international or intercultural experience has on young people. While studies investigating this have primarily been undertaken with university-aged students, there has been increasing interest in the impact on younger students as well. But this has been, and will continue to be, a difficult line of research to carry out, as much of the impact is not realized, nor measurable, until many years after someone has had an experience.

The experience abroad, regardless of the level at which it takes place, engages the student holistically, the entire process involving both physical and psychological transitions that impact the cognitive, affective, and behavioral domains. And, as was presented in chapter 6, these transitions occur twice, once during entry into the host culture and then again upon reentry into the home culture.

One of the goals of study abroad has always been to influence students' knowledge base, and several studies report impact in the cognitive domain. The majority of students who live and study abroad, for instance, report that their intercultural sojourn challenged their perceptions of themselves as well as of other Americans (see Cushner and Karim 2004 for a comprehensive survey of the research literature on study abroad). Those who have studied abroad for a semester or longer typically demonstrate an increase in cultural and political knowledge and display more analytical attitudes toward the host culture and more positive attitudes toward the self after the experience. When they return, these students tend to enroll in a greater number of foreign language classes and study these languages longer, spend a greater amount of time studying in college, and tend to be higher-achieving students after their experience than students who do not go abroad.

Intercultural sensitivity, personal autonomy, and openness to cultural diversity are also enhanced as a result of study abroad. Students who study overseas demonstrate higher levels of cross-cultural interest and cultural cosmopolitanism than do those who remain at home. In addition, participants also develop more positive, but more critical, attitudes toward their own country.

There is some documented long-term impact of the experience as well. Years later, people who have studied and lived abroad generally report having a greater understanding of the intellectual life and traditions of their host country in addition to an increased awareness of the differences between nations. Former study-abroad participants tend to become involved in more international activities; have more friends, professional colleagues, and acquaintances in other countries; and read more books and newspapers in foreign languages than do those who remained at home. Long-term impact on career advancement and personal accomplishments has also been associated with study abroad. Teachers who study abroad, for instance, return with a new sense of authority and a greater desire to share their knowledge and experience; have greater academic prestige because of their participation in an overseas program; and are more likely to apply and be selected for additional opportunities for international travel and study.

There is impact on the affective domain as well. Early studies that looked at the impact of study abroad demonstrated that participants report growth in independence and self-reliance and an increased ability to make decisions on their own. Significant changes in people's tolerance and understanding of other people and their views also occur as a result of study abroad. There is also evidence of an increase in self-confidence, adaptability, flexibility, and confidence in speaking to strangers and in gathering information in new and unfamiliar settings.

Those who participate in study-abroad programs also demonstrate greater levels of cultural sensitivity and racial consciousness, thus making them more effective at addressing domestic diversity issues as well. One of the most influential researchers in the field of prejudice formation and reduction, Thomas Pettigrew (2001), reviewed more than 200 studies of ethnic contact, of which one-fourth involved international contact through travel and student exchange. Excluding the relatively restricted encounters that are typical of most tourist experiences, international contact was shown to have a greater impact on reducing prejudice than does within-nation interethnic contact. Thus, student exchanges, especially those a semester or longer in duration, appear to be especially effective at achieving this end.

Behaviors may also change as a result of an international experience. For many, the overseas experience gives new direction and focus to their career paths. Some may wish to prepare for a career working with other sojourners and consider working as a foreign student counselor or international program adviser. Others may seek out careers that allow for subsequent international experiences, perhaps in the travel industry. Some find that the overseas experience has sensitized them to issues and values they never knew they held and find themselves studying environmental or political issues. And others work to internationalize whatever career they choose, becoming global or multicultural educators, international businesspeople, or Foreign Service officers. Others simply become good cultural mediators in their schools and communities, bringing their overseas experience to the domestic front for the benefit of others.

But some surprises have been observed that also need to be considered. Although many studies have found that exchange program participants decrease their ethnic distance or prejudice toward others significantly more than those who stay at home, some studies report that some participants become more xenophobic, or fearful of foreigners, and return home with a reinforced appreciation of their own homeland at the expense of the host nation. One reason for this may be that some programs are designed in such a way that participants spend far more time with their fellow students from home than they spend having new cultural experiences and intellectual engagement with host nationals. While such programs can be exciting, and students can experience a significant amount of travel, the outcome can be quite different.

Gmelch (1997), for instance, studied a group of fifty-one American students in a European university semester program, asking them to document their activities during the days when they left their program site to travel—typically via Eurail Pass on Fridays through Sundays. When asked, students believed that they learned more from their travel experiences on weekends than from their formal educational program.

What they actually experienced and learned, however, was quite different from what they thought they learned. The typical student tended to hop around the continent, spending more time traveling in trains than anything else, and averaged 1.72 countries and 2.4 cities per weekend over the six-week program, hoping to see as much as he or she could in the brief time available. On an average weekend, students spent 18.7 hours on trains and 3 hours in stations waiting for them—instead of staying in one place for the entire weekend and gaining more understanding of a particular area. Train schedules often determined where students went next, especially if they were not happy with a current destination. Whichever train left earliest was often the one that was chosen, regardless of where it was headed!

Even at the base study site, going out in large groups, which many seemed to do, prevented interaction with locals. After a few weeks, some students began to recognize the disadvantage of traveling in large groups and restricting their interactions to their own little community—in essence segregating themselves from locals. By traveling in large groups, students lessened the educational impact of their experience, and some realized that the experiences they had when alone or with only one other allowed them to focus more on their surroundings and people. When students do not make the effort to separate themselves from the larger group, they may not learn as much about local culture as is assumed by their parents and instructors. Instead, students engage rather superficially with the local culture and have little meaningful contact with locals.

Study trips, and in this case programs that allow for easy segregation from the local community, are not a substitute for independent or group travel that focuses on intercultural development. Surface-level encounters or programs where participants remain in relatively homogeneous and segregated groups do not seem to provide the depth of interpersonal engagement required for significant impact to occur. And to reiterate, major changes in knowledge and perception tend not to occur in the standard cognitive approach of the typical school experience.

THE ROLE OF EXPERIENCE IN INTERCULTURAL EDUCATION

It is one thing to read or hear from others that in some parts of the world it is common for men or women to hold hands with one another in public, not necessarily as a display of a same-sex relationship, but merely as a sign of friendship. I, for one, learned this piece of information when I was young and first traveling, found it quite intriguing, and would use it liberally in orientation sessions for would-be travelers. It was something quite different, however, when Mohammed, my Israeli Arab colleague referred to in chapter 7, suddenly took my hand as we walked along the streets in his village of Iksal. I just was not prepared for this act of friendship. Here he was, letting others in his village know that I, an outsider and an American Jew no less, was a trusted and true friend and should be welcomed in the community. Unfortunately, that was not the attribution I made the first time it happened. This just was not a behavior I was accustomed to, and I quickly removed my hand from his.

Thus, while I may have "learned" this fact cognitively from a book or lecture and could readily share this fact with others, it meant something quite different to me when it happened in real life. It was then, and only then, that I truly learned what this meant. Now, after some time, I can comfortably walk holding hands with Mohammed, and it's others who have to find their own meaning in our behavior.

Such is the crux of experiential learning: it is characterized by experiences that are affective and personal in nature. And it is critical to cross-cultural learning. Although technology increasingly makes it possible for people to be in almost instantaneous communication with one another, research continues to point to the critical role that firsthand, person-to-person immersion experiences play in helping people become more effective in their intercultural understanding. Experiential learning involves both the right and left hemispheres of the brain holistically, linking encounter with cognition. The international travel experience plays a major role in the success of this effort—there is just no substitute for the real thing.

Two other characteristics are often associated with experiential cross-cultural learning: it is planned and then pondered or thought about. Herein lies the role of the teacher. Distinct from a simple cross-cultural encounter, cross-cultural experiential learning, as Angene Wilson (1987) describes, is planned and reflected upon. An increasingly important task for educators today is to encourage and provide significant intercultural experiences for students and future teachers who typically are not experienced in cross-cultural matters. Teachers are a critical link in structuring educational experiences that help students reach out to the international community, both at home and abroad, with the aim of forging relationships based on deep and meaningful understandings of people's similarities as well as differences.

If we truly are serious about preparing teachers, and subsequently the pupils in their charge, to better understand the complex world in which we live and to develop the skills necessary to interact effectively with people from a variety of cultural backgrounds, then understanding the manner in which people learn about culture becomes critical. If teachers are truly architects of educational experiences and opportunity, they must understand how closely cognition and experience, or affect, are intertwined—they are just inseparable when it comes to culture learning. A deep understanding and commitment to living and working with others is not achieved in a cognitive-only approach to learning; it develops only with attention to experience and the affective domain. It is through experiential, immersion-type experiences that young people are challenged to make sense of their new environment and accommodate any changes required for them to better survive, ultimately gaining a feeling of being at home in a new context and becoming more knowledgeable about other people.

Unfortunately, Merryfield (2000) suggests that most teachers have not been prepared to teach for diversity and do not understand the impact of globalization on the lives of their students and communities. Interested in understanding why this is so, Merryfield interviewed eighty teacher educators recognized by their peers for their success in preparing teachers in both multicultural and global education. What she discovered is of importance to this entire book. There are significant differences between the experiences of people of color and those who are white that reflect the importance of experiential learning.

Most American teachers of color have a double consciousness (DuBois 1989). That is, many have grown up conscious not only of their own primary culture, but also of having experienced discrimination and outsider status, through their encounters with a society characterized by white privilege and racism. Middle-class white teacher educators who were effective at teaching for diversity had their most profound and influential experiences while living outside their own country as an expatriate. These teachers had encountered discrimination and exclusion by being an outsider within another cultural context.

As Merryfield's study suggests, those who leave the comfort of their home society for an extended period of time come to understand what it is like to live outside the mainstream and to be perceived as "the other." It is the influential international experience that has thus helped many European American mainstream teachers become more ethnorelative in their understanding of others, more skilled at crossing cultures, and committed to bringing about change through their work. Thus, for many, travel leads to new, firsthand understanding of what it means to be marginalized and to be a victim of stereotypes and prejudice, and how this might affect people.

Travel also affords people the opportunity to experience both what happens to their identity when they are no longer in control and the contradictions between their beliefs, expectations, and knowledge and the multiple realities of others (Merryfield 2000). Reconciling these disconfirmed expectations in a real-life context forces people to reflect and question, thus deconstructing previously held assumptions or knowledge about themselves as well as others. Thus, the international lived experience sets the stage for developing a consciousness of multiple realities and serves as the stimulus that prompts new learning.

A strong rationale for integrating international travel into education can be found in the context of situative theory (Putnam and Borko 2000).

Since so much of learning occurs within the confines of a typical classroom setting, behaviors of both teachers and learners often become routine and automatic. In situative learning, the context in which the individual learns is seen as integral to one's cognition. Outside experiences and encounters facilitate the individual development of alternative perspectives, thus helping people see themselves as global citizens and others as potential partners. The outside experiences encountered through international educational travel provide the necessary context for this to occur.

Traveling as a tourist—be it individually, in small groups, or even in the more common large groups in which school groups often travel—is qualitatively different from the kinds of experiences that are possible in carefully guided educationally focused travel. Casual travel through tourism involves an educational component that, although theoretically possible, is rarely achieved (Li 2000). Tourists traveling in groups may travel in a world unto their own, surrounded by, but not necessarily integrated into, the host society. The casual tourist experience is typically understood through the eyes of tour guides, tourist brochures, commercial guidebooks, and programmed performances that typically sanitize and generalize the local culture as if tourists were spectators at a sporting event, visually consuming their destination rather than fully engaging with it. Meaning is generally made and communicated by others, not the self.

Humans, as social beings, learn best in situations where the complexity of social reality is encountered, examined, and understood. Such is the nature of constructivist learning. In the situated learning that occurs in a well-structured international travel experience, the context enables learners to participate in the social milieu of the host setting, allowing them to build rapport with locals, interpersonal relationships with host families, and identification with a local community. Mass tourism does not allow this to occur and may simply distort and reinforce stereotypical images of many of the world's peoples. Travel sets the stage for people to engage in meaningful relationships and thus opens up opportunities that may otherwise not occur. Through interpersonal dialogue and personal encounters, people have the opportunity to learn to see others, as well as themselves, through new eyes. It is just not possible to recreate the critical relational interdependence of the learner, the activity, and the world in the formal classroom setting.

The lived experience is thus the critical element in gaining a meaningful understanding of other cultures as well as one's own place in an interconnected world. Although the process of learning a second culture is in some ways similar to that of learning one's original culture, it is significantly different in many respects. When one is learning one's original culture, the entire surroundings, including family, community, and institutions, support such efforts, and there is little discontinuity between what one already knows and what one is expected to learn. In learning a second culture, one comes into immediate conflict between the culture of self and the new culture to which one is exposed. Reconciling these differences is critical to successful adjustment and subsequent learning.

In any new cultural setting, the individual is confronted with continuous tensions between new information and behavior that must be accommodated and previously learned knowledge and information that must be eliminated or temporarily ignored. Suddenly, in the new setting, new categories of information must be identified and understood, and in many cases, finer differentiations must be made in categories that were once not seen as important or that may not have even existed. Problems must be solved in settings that are new to the individual, without the supports one has come to depend upon. Thus, large-group travel should not be a substitute for independent travel. Students should be encouraged to travel in small numbers because doing so increases the likelihood of interacting with local people and having to solve daily problems.

Piaget and Inhelder (1958) suggest that when individuals travel, changes in their environment cause them to acquire new understanding about life, culture, and themselves. Individual change and maturation occurs during periods of discontinuity, displacement, and disjunction. Conversely, little change occurs when people are in a state of equilibrium.

As emphasized by the eighteen-theme culture-general framework (Cushner and Brislin 1996), one's emotions, while initially unanticipated, are oftentimes highly engaged in a new cultural setting. One can retreat to one's own culture, either by returning home or by segregating oneself from the local people. Or one can begin taking the risks necessary to learn new behaviors that will facilitate one's integration into the local ways. If one chooses to remain and learn in the new setting, especially with the guidance of a good educator, it becomes increasingly impossible to achieve an emotional distance from the surroundings. Emotional engagement is thus a critical element in the learning process because it prompts one to pause, observe, hypothesize, reflect, and inquire. Sikkema and Niyekawa (1987) concur when they state that it is the "emotional ego-involving experience of success and failure as well as the temporary loss of role identity that makes the learning from living in another culture different from learning about the culture from lectures, books, films, and simulated experiences" (p. 43).

But it is through reflection that people make meaning of what they have encountered. Thus, while experiences outside one's own culture provide the necessary foundation from which further learning can occur, they cannot stand alone. Each stage of the educational travel experience—planning and preparation, travel to the destination, the in-context experience, return home, and reflection and evaluation—becomes an essential element of any learning that takes place. But, different from a tourist experience, where learning, if it occurs, is incidental and haphazard, in the educational travel experience, facilitation of learning by a teacher should take place at each step along the way. The teacher thus becomes a critical dimension of effective culture learning as he or she considers all stages of travel. Guiding observation, reflection, interpretation, and application are all essential functions of the teacher.

⑩

BUILDING TRUST, RELATIONSHIPS, AND COMMITMENT, EVEN THOUGH SOMETIMES THINGS GO WRONG

> The sea is dangerous and its storms terrible, but these obstacles have never been sufficient reason to remain ashore.
>
> —Ferdinand Magellan

Reflect back to that game warden discussion where this book began. Recall that Joy and George Adamson devoted much of their time to preparing the young of various animal species, primarily lions who had been orphaned or abandoned, to survive on their own. Patiently gaining the trust of their students, the Adamsons provided countless opportunities for them to practice and learn survival skills and gain independence so that they could ultimately venture out on their own. This is not unlike what parents and teachers of our own species struggle to accomplish with their own children and students. The Adamsons, like some parents, were not always successful, however. Sometimes their students, like our own children, were hours late returning, worrying them to no end. At other times, they simply did not return—perhaps they were injured, got lost, went off on their own, got into trouble, or were killed by predators or hunters. But the Adamsons did not stop their efforts, even though there were setbacks along the way.

When similar concerns are encountered with our own young, should we keep them from exploring, from venturing out to spread their wings in an attempt to better understand their world and become peacemakers? Things don't always go as planned, and sometimes the pain and loss experienced in the process can be hard to endure. In such circumstances, we need to remember the grand plan, the purpose for these efforts and activities. No individual or society ever grew or developed without some loss and pain along the way to maturity.

Unfortunate circumstances would form the backdrop of my experience when I returned to Africa about thirty years after my first visit to the continent. It was six in the morning when the Swissair flight I was traveling on from Zurich landed in Jomo Kenyatta International Airport in Nairobi. The capital city had already come to life, and by the time I was traveling along the highway, the streets were teeming with people on their way to school and work. Twelve marabou storks that were perched atop large acacia trees greeted us as we entered the city limits. Where else in the world can one be welcomed with fantastic wildlife right within the city limits? Even Nairobi National Park, located just eight miles from the city center, can provide the lucky visitor with a photograph of a rhinoceros, with the Nairobi skyline as a backdrop.

The driver had met me as planned and was to take me to the bus terminal in time for a 9:00 A.M. bus. From Nairobi, I was to travel about six hours southeast toward Mombasa, requesting to be dropped off in the town of Maungu, about thirty kilometers past the regional center, Voi. Someone, I was assured, would pick me up.

The Taita Discovery Centre, or TDC, located in a corridor between Tsavo East and Tsavo West National Parks, would be my home for four weeks while I served as a volunteer, learning some of the skills of a wildlife researcher. Staff at TDC were most interested in understanding what might be done to improve the situation for the estimated one thousand elephants and few hundred lions that use the area as a corridor as they migrate between the two parks. TDC is a comprehensive conservation project that includes study and collaboration with a number of communities directly affected by the elephants. I would assist with some elephant research, help develop a curriculum project, explore possible linkages with American schools and universities, and perhaps bring a group of students or teachers here for school and community experiences in the Kenyan bush. It promised to be just the right blend of bush life, wildlife work, and community involvement, and a test of the importance of trust and mutual understanding to the success of long-term relationships and collaborative work.

I usually try to avoid traveling by bus, at least in the United States, having grown up hearing about all kinds of horrible things that supposedly have happened on them. There seemed to be pride in the station here; when I arrived, they were sweeping the street clean—and it was a dirt road. Already quite tired of sitting after the overnight plane ride, I stood for more than an hour before the bus was ready to depart, waiting patiently in an area only large enough to hold three or four passengers. The eight-hour ride would take us past a number of small towns and marketplaces on its way to Mombasa, the bus stopping only occasionally to pick up or drop off passengers. Nothing to eat or drink was available on the bus, and I was not told this before I left. This didn't seem to be such a big deal because I'd been awake and eating all night on the flight from Europe. Anyway, as a vegetarian, I had protein food bars handy in case I grew hungry. There also was no toilet on the bus, and I was not prepared for this either.

Although we seemed to stop at every town and village along the way as more and more people got on board, no rest stop was apparent. About two hours into the trip, which was now about four hours after I had left the airport, I began to feel those lower twinges that remind me that I have a bladder—and at my age this is something I generally pay attention to. I really had no idea if the bus had any planned stops where we could get off, but I sat patiently, hoping my worst fears would not materialize.

Another half hour into the trip and my worst fears seemed to be coming true. I now had to pee really badly! Fidgeting nervously in my seat, I tried all kinds of things—from loosening my belt and holding my waist to mind control—anything to relieve the pressure on my bladder. I even began to wonder if it was possible to dribble a little urine down my leg every minute or so. I had read that this is something quite common in the region—at least among young male elephants when they are in the condition known as musth and they constantly dribble strong-smelling urine to mark their territory and announce that they are in their prime. Well, I certainly was long past my prime, and I wouldn't go out of my way to advertise what I was doing, but perhaps releasing a small amount now and then would not be noticed—or considered offensive—by my seatmate who joined me at the last stop. And given the heat of the day, evaporation would quickly take care of the evidence.

After a bit more time the bus stopped, seemingly in the middle of nowhere. Two people got up, a man in the front and a woman sitting right behind me, and quickly ran off the bus, he running toward a bush. I glanced around, asked my seatmate if this was a toilet stop, and, following a nod of reassurance, quickly joined the other two in the bushes. It was awkward, to say the least, as I stood next to this man, trying to relax enough to pee into the bushes, with thirty or more of my fellow passengers looking on. And it was confusing as well because only ten minutes earlier I had read in my travel book that it is considered uncouth to urinate in public in Kenya. Later I would learn that this was referred to as the "bush room" and was quite common where I would be spending my time. As I turned to get back on the bus, there was the woman, her dress lifted to her waist, squatting alongside the back tire. We glanced briefly at each other. I think I noticed a little tinkle, or was that twinkle, in her eye.

The bus continued on, dropping me off in Maungu, and someone from TDC did come to get me, but only after I had waited more than an hour and a half; no one knew that I had been put on the earlier bus. Afraid to venture too far from the intersection where the bus left me, I waited patiently in the searing sun and red dust that would soon become a part of every day, making friends and chitchatting with the cows and kids, both human and goat, that kept passing by to get a look at this new *mzungu*, or European, in their midst.

This was my welcome back to Africa—and it can challenge the most seasoned of travelers, especially those not traveling on first-class tickets or staying in five-star hotels. Not long after their arrival on the continent, usually within the first twenty-four to forty-eight hours, most people will face their challenge in Africa. Whether that challenge is confronting new foods, uncertain water, anxieties about the wildlife, fear of illness, excessive poverty, or potential for thievery; working through bureaucratic red tape; or participating in the everyday frustrations of the people, Africa can try even the hardiest of souls. The traveler in Africa is truly on a safari—a journey, as it translates from the Kiswahili—that can be as much an external adventure as it is an internal transformative venture. I had touched the continent a few times in the past, and certainly many years earlier in my dreams, and it had touched me. I was glad to be back.

The Taita Discovery Centre is located within a 170,000-acre tract in the Taru Desert, within the Taita and Rukinga ranches, at the base of Mount Kasigau. This is a semiarid region, and I found it quite dry and dusty, even given the fact that I had arrived just a few weeks after the short rains. The area lies, along with sixteen other ranches, in the corridor between Tsavo East and Tsavo West National Parks—the largest of the national park systems in all of Kenya. There is a history of poaching, especially of the elephants throughout the area. In 1973, Kenya had an elephant population estimated to be at 167,000. By 1989, the population had been reduced to 17,000. Even with the worldwide ban on the sale of ivory, poaching, especially in this region, was still common. There may be a grain of truth to the saying that elephants never forget. Because of their relatively recent experiences with poachers, elephants are understandably quite skittish around humans and oftentimes difficult to find. This area is being studied with the hope of reestablishing it as an active, healthy, safe region for wildlife—especially for the elephants that migrate within the corridor between the two parks. The Taita Discovery Centre lies at the heart of this effort.

Studying wildlife is not the same as the game viewing that most visitors to Africa experience. Game viewing is more like a game of bingo in the bush. Small groups of camera-laden tourists typically go off in six-passenger minivans in search of the "big five": lion, elephant, buffalo, rhinoceros, and leopard. The trip is generally not considered a success until all five have been seen and photographed—BINGO! Next in importance come such animals as cheetahs, baboons, hippopotamuses, crocodiles, wildebeests, giraffes, and zebras, among others. They are large, impressive, and photogenic, and I must admit to spending much of my time in search of the award-winning photo. Although I've won no awards, I am nonetheless pleased with many of the photos I have taken.

But game viewing in and of itself is not sufficient if we are to succeed in our efforts to conserve this magnificent resource. While this activity may bring greater awareness of the splendor of these creatures to an increasing number of people around the world, the more hidden day-to-day struggles these animals face, including their interactions with human populations, are little understood.

Such are the concerns of the wildlife researchers and many of the volunteers associated with TDC, of which I was now one. Wildlife researchers at TDC, especially those studying the elephant, struggle to make themselves as inconspicuous as possible, sitting quietly for hours on end, waiting for the drama of life to unfold so that it can be documented and later analyzed. When game viewing, if nothing is seen within a short period of time, one quickly moves on to another site, with drivers in constant radio communication with one another in search of the large game—and the big tips from satisfied clients. It is not uncommon in the parks to find that within a few minutes of one group locating a lion or cheetah, van after van arrives, encircling the animal, making it nearly impossible for anyone to capture a photo without also snaring a bumper, window, or other camera lens as well. So much for the isolation of nature.

I quickly learned that research in support of wildlife is not always filled with the glamour of Joy and George Adamson's struggles with Elsa the lioness that had motivated my early longings for Africa. Because it is the little things that are important, patience, and oftentimes loneliness, becomes the researcher's constant companion. Without an unlimited supply, the work soon fails.

I was introduced to the demands of this work, and the efforts of TDC, on my first full day on-site, when I was invited to participate with a small team to do animal counts at three dams that were originally constructed to provide water for the cattle grazing within the ranches. Efforts are under way to eliminate ranching from the area, and wildlife is now using an increasing number of these water holes. The dams were to be monitored for three hours each day for three days of every month over the next three years to determine the animal life that was dependent upon them.

The difficulty of this work was made clear to me from our very first visit to a dam—it had no water! There we sat, for three hours at a time at three dams: one that had no water, one that had less than 10 percent of its capacity, and one that, although it appeared full, was frequented by hundreds of cattle, sheep, goats, and people on a fairly regular basis, with the result that wildlife was kept at a distance. We sat as if patiently awaiting God's theater to begin, and I expected to see countless large animals. In the three days of monitoring water holes we saw a total of three warthogs and three dik-diks, the smallest antelope to be found on the African savannah, who themselves do not even drink! We logged countless birds, however, many of which I had never seen before. Rather useless in terms of my contribution to the project as I knew very little about the birdlife, I busied myself serving as secretary as often as possible to keep from falling asleep, and reading a book on elephant communication. And I slowly began to learn about the birds.

Hamisi Mutinda was head of conservation and animal research when I first ventured to TDC. A conservationist who recently completed his doctoral dissertation on the social relationships of elephants, he is soft-spoken, determined, focused, and devoted. Hamisi had been working with a group of young British volunteers in the weeks before I joined TDC. These young people, most of them between the ages of eighteen and nineteen, had come to Kenya after graduating high school but before beginning college to volunteer for four months in the local communities. They had recently completed their orientation at TDC and had begun their time in the local communities.

Hamisi has devoted his life to working on behalf of the African elephant. While he has always been interested in wildlife and believed that people and animals can coexist, it wasn't until 1988 that he became motivated to do something about it. At the funeral of a distant relative, he met a woman who was willing to pay poachers anything to rid her *shamba*, or farm, of elephants, complaining that they did nothing but destroy everything she planted. This was his wake-up call, so to speak; he decided that if this woman could be so committed to ridding the world of elephants, he could be as dedicated to their preservation. He hasn't looked back since and had worked with the Kenya Wildlife Service as well as with well-known elephant researcher Cynthia Moss and her project at the Amboseli National Park before joining the staff at TDC.

One of the conservationists' biggest struggles is finding alternative economic sources for the people in the area who have traditionally been dependent upon livestock or harvesting crops from their shambas for their income base. Most locals have little interest in wildlife; it invades their physical and economic space, and they reap few of the benefits from tourism. The problem is complex and multifaceted, and conservationists struggle to balance economic incentives with value for the local population by not interfering with their traditional way of life. But this work is slow, and Hamisi worries that people will not leave the land fast enough to save the elephants.

My real contribution to the work of TDC, which I am told is of equal importance, lies in community–school relationships. Such efforts, Hamisi insists, are a critical dimension of this work. Trust between TDC and local communities must be established, and at the same time, people must be provided with the knowledge and skills that will enable and encourage them to be less dependent upon the land and more tolerant of elephants. It seems that I may have found the right combination of passion and profession to work for me; I can bring my skills as an educator to the support of the elephant.

I was assured that there were many large animals in the region, some of them quite dangerous, but as of day 6, I really had only spotted a few here and there. And I was somewhat disappointed, to be honest, because this really was what I had come to see, as do many others who venture to the continent. People are drawn to the drama of the chase, hoping to witness the life-and-death struggle that is so much a part of Africa. This also serves as a reminder of our animal roots, a reminder that we, too, are really an integral part of the natural cycle of things. But while we hope to witness this as a passive observer and not as an integral part of the chain of events, this is not always the case, as I was to discover during my stay.

On the morning of the seventh day we are to go off elephant monitoring. That is, we are to travel across the property in search of elephants that can be spotted, identified, and recorded—again, in order to gain greater understanding of the range and population of these great beasts. It is easiest to locate elephants or any of the animals during the dry season since they tend to congregate at the water holes to satisfy their thirst, which, depending upon the species, can vary from once a day to once every three days or more. Hamisi collaborates with other researchers who have been tracking elephants for years to determine which elephants have also been spotted in the neighboring Tsavo Parks. We depart, equipped with boxes of elephant ID cards, which note unique ear notches and tears and tusk formations that are used to identify and thus differentiate one elephant from another. The elephants are also given names—such as Shiloh, Patty, and Hesse—and I have the chance to name quite a few over the weeks.

We arrive at Kongoni water hole at about 8:30 in the morning. After circling the water we notice recent elephant activity and decide to stay. Positioning ourselves with a view of the water and surrounding area, we turn off the engine and begin our long wait, something I became accustomed to while monitoring water holes the previous week. Our presence has chased most everything away: there is hardly a sound or evidence of activity during the first half hour. Hamisi warns us not to take photos until the elephants, assuming there will be some, begin drinking and making their own sounds that drown out the noise our cameras make.

I sit atop our four-wheel-drive Land Cruiser and wait in quiet meditation with Mount Kasigau as the backdrop. The parched red earth, sparse vegetation, and dry heat are reminders of just how precious these water holes are for all the living creatures. If animals are to survive in this environment, especially during the dry spells, they must eventually come here; these are not mirages. The air remains quiet, with only a few birds beginning to chirp and break the silence.

Although we are out tracking elephants, it is the smaller life forms that keep us engaged. We busy ourselves observing some of the more than 160 species of birds found in Kenya, among them the colorful Eurasian roller, perhaps an unwelcome seasonal migrant from Europe that we have observed in apparent competition for similar resources with the local drongo. There are also countless hornbills, a few extravagant secretary birds strutting around, and more than a dozen colorful bee-eaters that dart through the air. The sound of my pen on my notebook competes with the sounds of the birds as we continue to wait.

An hour passes, with the temperature increase causing the sweat to pour from my body. Although it is only 9:30 in the morning, I am completely covered to protect my face and neck from the sun. While this only makes me sweat more profusely, it is a necessary precaution for my sun-sensitive skin in this desert environment. Ever so slowly the scene changes and I begin to lose all sense of time. A small group of Burchell's zebras warily emerges from the brush. After a few minutes we count six in all. Cautiously surveying the area for predators or any other threat, they pay particular attention to our vehicle across the water. Pulling back both their upper and lower lips, they show their bottom and top teeth, a sign that they are investigating our presence. We are thus rewarded for our patience.

But there is more to come. It is obvious that this spot sees much elephant activity as there is evidence of dung piles, many from a few weeks ago and some that are more recent, perhaps left only yesterday. Footprints of all sizes seem frozen in the mud and along the shore, and the air is full with a sweet odor characteristic of elephants. Suddenly, and without any auditory warning, we see one large female begin to emerge from the right. She hesitates briefly, raising her trunk high to sniff the air. Apparently satisfied, she continues to lumber toward us as eight others follow closely behind. This is a cow and calf group, with four adults and subadults accompanying five calves that we estimate to be between one year and four years of age. It is surprising how quiet such a large animal can be. When they are not breaking branches or pulling leaves, you would have no idea they were on the march.

The calves begin to move toward the water's edge until the matriarch, who typically brings up the rear, rushes forward, nudging the entire group to continue on. Perhaps she has spotted fresher water or wishes the young to enter from more stable ground. Regardless of the reason, it is obvious who is in charge. The group stops opposite our vehicle and the elephants, like the zebras, stare closely at us until they are comfortable enough to continue. They work their way to their favored spot, luckily in better view for us. The group drinks from the water, we take our photos, and they begin playing and bathing nearby. The zebras have yet to step toward the water.

Vocal communication plays a major part in communication among social creatures, and elephants are no exception. Having rather limited vocalization, however, elephants keep in touch with one another by making low growls that were first thought to be stomach rumbles. Females are capable of making twenty-two different sounds, while males produce only seven; you are free to pose your own hypothesis as to why this might be so. But for years, it was obvious to many that elephants seemed to have a sixth sense. That is, they appeared to communicate with one another over vast distances without making sounds, causing some scientists to suggest that elephants used ESP.

It is now known that in addition to the low sounds that are heard among elephants, they also produce a number of sounds that are inaudible to the human ear. Thus, a significant amount of communication by elephants is carried out through infrasound at a subsonic level more than an octave below the level humans can hear. Because of their low frequency, these sounds travel great distances in the bush and may be heard by other elephants up to six kilometers away. Elephants that are well out of sight of others in their family grouping can thus remain in constant contact using infrasound to coordinate their activities.

We should not be surprised when from our left enters a rather large male, and from just behind us a young male. The young male is startled when he spots us. Somewhat threatened, he turns toward us, throws back his head and ears, trumpets a warning our way, and struts around a bit. This causes a slight adrenaline rush in me, but it soon subsides. Hamisi reminds us of the stressful experiences these elephants have had around humans and that in this early stage of the project we are working to recognize the elephants while building trust among them. With time they will become accustomed to human presence. Backing away, our new arrival finds a spot between us and the cow–calf group, rarely taking his eyes from us. The slow building of trust seems as critical to the success of working with wildlife as it does to working with people of different communities.

At about the age of twelve, male elephants begin to mature and typically travel apart from the cow–calf groups. Although not yet socially mature for another eight to ten years, they enter a state called musth when they become sexually active. During musth, males seek out females in heat. The arrival of our two males is probably not a coincidence but perhaps the result of hearing through infrasound that the cow–calf group was to be at the water hole. The males are here to check out the females—perhaps they are not much different from our own species in this way. As there appear to be no females in reproductive readiness in this group, our male visitors depart shortly after completing their drink.

They do not go too far, however, and they circle our vehicle, perhaps to threaten us once again out of frustration since their sexual longings have not been satisfied. The air suddenly erupts with a frightening sound as one of the males finds a convenient way to scratch his side—and a nearby acacia tree begins swaying back and forth. Both males continue to hang around the water hole; perhaps they have sensed another group approaching and wish to see if any of the females are sexually receptive.

Then, almost as quickly as the elephants appeared, they seem ready to depart. The cow–calf group leaves from the opposite side of the water hole from which they arrived. Like an adolescent boy teasing a girl in the school halls, one of the males follows the cow–calf group in hot pursuit—perhaps hoping that one of the females is, in fact, in heat. The entire group of females seems bothered by his persistent presence, however, as they trot off in the distance. The zebras now feel confident enough to approach for their drink, and then they, too, are gone. Although it stays quiet for some time, we remain throughout the day, having had much practice sitting still, hoping to avoid "economy-class syndrome" in our four-wheel-drive vehicles.

Our day ends with yet another treat. A lone giraffe slowly approaches as the sun begins to set, and we are rewarded with a scene many visitors never have a chance to witness. Like the zebras earlier in the day, this giraffe is cautious, taking most of an hour, slowly moving toward the water and checking from side to side each step of the way.

While its height is a marvelous adaptation for browsing among the tops of acacia trees and for sighting potential danger, it is a liability when it comes to drinking. This dance to drink challenges the giraffe more than any other animal. While all animals are vulnerable at the water hole, the giraffe has the most concern, both in terms of its safety and the effect that gravity plays on its blood pressure. For the giraffe, there is the potential danger of the brain being damaged each time it lowers its head, as when a person has a stroke. While the giraffe has evolved various adaptations to prevent this from happening, it also explains why the animal is reluctant to lower its head too far.

We watch in awe as our giraffe begins to slowly and awkwardly splay its legs out, one at a time, gaining that sensitive balance that will allow it to lower its head to the water to drink. The water level at this particular spot, however, is about six inches lower than the edge of the water hole, and it is just too far for our giraffe to manage. He catches himself, almost falling forward into the water. Changing his strategy, he moves farther down the water's edge, peering in every direction, as he saunters slowly toward our vehicle. He is successful at this next attempt. As he finishes drinking, he sways his head, pendulum-like, using the impetus generated by this motion to help lift the front of his body, bring his front legs together, and thus regain his upright posture. He slowly departs into the darkness.

The long rains begin within a week of my arrival. It's amazing how after a couple of days of good rain this semiarid region is dramatically altered. Along with the burst of greenery, flowers, and pollen—hence my allergies—come the young of many of the animals and an onslaught of insects I have yet to see. I am most leery of the mosquitoes and the threat of malaria, even though I am taking my dose of Larium religiously at 7:00 A.M. each Tuesday morning. At night, it is sometimes difficult to tell if the insects are inside or outside the mosquito net since the buzzing seems to be relentless. Some nights I must unknowingly press up against the net as I sleep, for I awake each morning with fresh bites on my arms and legs.

Although we were able to observe animals at nearby water holes in my first week at TDC, now that the rains have come and small basins of water collect almost everywhere on the property, there is no need for them to converge at the few water sources available. It thus becomes increasingly difficult to locate animals for extensive study, so it is the perfect time for me to shift my focus from the bush to the local communities. I welcome the opportunity to begin work in the schools.

Five communities make up the Nyangala cluster of schools at the base of Mount Kasigau: Kiteghe, Rukanga, Jora, Bungule, and Makwasinyi. It is within these communities that the British volunteers work, assisting in a variety of community projects. I plan to seek the assistance of these young people while working with the schools. Among the volunteers is a young girl named Amy. It is easy to see why she is so well liked by the villagers in Bungule where she resides. She is vibrant, animated, open, and outgoing—just the attributes required of one who has to integrate into a culturally different community for only a brief period of time. Amy is among the easiest of the sixteen volunteers for me to get to know, reminding me somewhat of my own eighteen-year-old daughter. A parent would be quite proud of her, pleased with the experience she is having and the contributions she is making before moving on to her university studies. As I write this, it is still hard to believe what happened to her.

Each of the communities has one primary school serving children in standards (grades) 1–8. While each school is meant to have one teacher per grade level regardless of the number of children in the school (and this varies from 157 to 350 students), some schools have only six teachers. There is also one secondary school, Moi High School, a boarding facility that serves about 180 children who can both pass the entrance exam and pay the $350 annual tuition.

I drive each day the one hour from TDC to Kasigau, using four-wheel-drive vehicles over roads that get worse with each rainfall. It takes the better part of each day to move between two schools, meet with the school head and teachers to discuss a possible curriculum project, and interact with the many children who are as interested in being with this mzungu as I am in being with them. After three days I have been introduced to key personnel at each school and am reminded of the time required to accomplish even the simplest of tasks—five thirty-minute meetings in three days. But spending this time is a critical element in the trust building that is essential if I expect to return with others to this vibrant region.

I have also come with a strategy to introduce myself as a newcomer. A few years ago I began traveling with a small Polaroid camera that allows me to snap photos of children, and sometimes their parents and teachers, hand them the print, and watch them wait in amazement as their image slowly appears on the paper. This works magic at warming people up to me and allows me to leave something with them. And for many, this may be the first time they have seen an image of themselves. I am now better able to enter their world, and they let me photograph them with my more sophisticated equipment. The children at the schools greet me on subsequent visits with huge smiles and repeated requests for "peek-tours!"

While here, I hope to begin a small curriculum project documenting the local culture and way of life. Since I cannot be in each of the schools every day, I seek the assistance of the British volunteers, training them to interview teachers and other villagers to collect information on the culture of the region. If I am successful at getting teachers to contribute, I can envision a more elaborate effort that would bring a group of American teachers to spend time in the communities, collaborate with local teachers in collecting information, and produce a major curriculum product about the Kasigau region to educate Americans about the links between conservation, culture, and community.

Change is slow, and teachers here have never been part of such a curriculum-writing effort. Their own history is not written down, and they

BUILDING TRUST, RELATIONSHIPS, AND COMMITMENT 137

have limited resources from which to teach. But the teachers are eager, and when I return a few days after our first meeting, many have rough notes already in hand.

Toward the end of my stay I spend a day doing women's work—but I'd be hard-pressed to convince my friends and colleagues at home that what I am doing is indeed women's work. The village of Makwasinyi is in the process of building a fishpond as an attempt to introduce fish farming to the region. This is one of the ways TDC is attempting to link conservation activities with the needs of the local communities. It is hoped that if small business enterprises are introduced and protein is provided for the community, people will be less dependent upon their own fields for crops and will avoid the tendency to poach game.

Parents from the community are encouraged to assist on this day, and about fifteen people show up to work; I am the only outsider. Significant differences are evident between me and the Kenyans I work alongside. Working hard, we sweat in the sun all morning, digging dirt and hauling it to provide support for the outside wall of the pond. It's amazing how well adapted people are to the local environment; I seem to be the only one who has to stop every twenty minutes in order to drink water. I also find it difficult to stop digging to complain about the sand in the bottom of my shoes: the women working beside me, hauling buckets of soil that each weigh at least twenty-five pounds, are barefoot, even among the scorpions that emerge from their holes every now and then. I guess if I weren't wearing shoes I wouldn't complain about having dirt in them either. I remove mine, but my feet are just too tender for the hard soil. I gain tremendous respect for these hard-working women.

Not all people are literate and able to share their stories in ways that allow others in the world to hear and learn. This certainly is the case in this region of Kenya—the entire history of the Taita people exists in the memories and oral traditions of the community, little of it written down to be shared with the young. Surprisingly, not only did my presence in Kenya result in me learning a tremendous amount, but my role as a teacher helped facilitate learning among the local community members as well.

The principal of Bungule school, the community in which Amy lived and worked, arranged for four of the village elders to meet one Sunday to discuss their early experiences. This was the moment we were hoping for since many different constituencies would be involved and benefit: the teachers, because they took the initiative to get the activity off the ground; the school, as it was an opportunity for parents, students, and community to come together; I, because we would videotape the encounter and have it translated from the Taita to both Kiswahili and English; and the elders themselves, who would be the center of attention as they shared their experiences and knowledge. This would hopefully be the spark that would start a major curriculum effort. We were to meet at 2:00 P.M. at the school on my last Sunday afternoon.

We arrived about 2:50, no one I was with seeming the least bit concerned that by my standards of timekeeping we were almost an hour late. When we pulled into the school, there, sitting beneath a 600-year-old baobab tree, were our four elders, and no one else. At first I was a bit disappointed, as I had hoped that at least some of the children and their families would attend the session. *Hakuna matata!* Not to worry! Sure enough, by the time we had set up the video camera and tape recorder a small crowd of about fifty people, both children and parents, had gathered. More would join us as the afternoon progressed.

We were introduced to our guests, Isaac Machonga, age 96; Thomas Kongere, age 71; Valey Kalaggi, age 96; and Constance Olijajabu, age 66. Valey had the strongest handshake I had encountered in some time—quite remarkable for a ninety-six-year-old woman. We asked them to relate what had happened to the Kasigau people during World War I. They shared a remarkable story about how the British troops had banished the Kasigau people from the area and sent them to the coastal region, where scores of them had died. It wasn't until many years later that they were allowed to return. This was the first time many of the young people in the audience had heard their own history.

A quiet remained over the audience when Isaac had finished telling his story. Someone then asked how life had changed over the years and what they missed from the old days. Valey talked about how marriage practices had changed.

"In the old times," she began, "fathers met and arranged the marriage between a boy and girl. Once an arrangement had been decided upon, the parents prepared a local beer to celebrate. But they did not tell the children that they were to be married. In most cases, girls were simply carried off late at night and taken to the boy's house."

Giggles erupted from all the young girls and many of the parents in the audience, as if this, too, were the first time many had heard of this practice.

Valey continued. "We didn't have wedding rings like they do today. And we didn't wear many clothes either; mostly some beads around our arms and perhaps a cloth around our waist. At the ceremony, castor oil was smeared on the legs of both the boy and the girl to announce the marriage."

Again, there were giggles from the audience. Valey stopped.

"What do you think young people today miss from the past?" I asked.

Thomas talked about how he missed major celebrations such as those of births and marriages. "We seem to miss much of the community building that we had in the old times, and I think this is a shame. We used to have big feasts to mark major events in our lives. Today, we do not do these things; Christianity has changed a lot of that, and we now celebrate religious holidays. But I think our young people miss out on much of our cultural ways. We also used to have initiation rites when we were boys and girls. We would go off with our age mates for about one week to learn what it took to become a man or a woman. We also had circumcision ceremonies, for both boys and girls, that are no longer practiced today. While people are still circumcised, today it is usually done by a doctor without the community's involvement. I think we are missing a lot, and our young people lose out."

"What did you learn in the initiation rites?" someone from the audience asked.

"I'm sorry, but I can't tell you that. We were warned that if we ever told others about what happened when we were initiated, we would dry up and end up like the dirt at your feet. None of us will ever tell what we did."

There were some giggles from the younger people.

"Even if that knowledge is lost forever because you no longer have the ceremony?" I asked.

"Even so," all four agreed.

The session lasted much longer than expected. When it ended I presented each of the elders with a kilogram of sugar and some tea as a token of appreciation for the time they gave us. But they, themselves, also appreciated the opportunity to share their stories and be the center of attention for a brief time, as did the community at large. There were many requests to repeat the event, and the heads from the other schools agreed to take up the charge. They would identify specific topics ahead of time so people could come better prepared. Witchcraft and religion seemed to be high on everyone's list.

Mornings in Africa are full of stories if one is able to read the signs left on the ground by the animals the previous evening. The evening sounds also tell a story all their own. One particular evening, the story was not pleasant.

A small group of us, two paying volunteers and a staff of four, was having a quiet dinner together at TDC, having returned late from the villages. The sixteen young British volunteers had spent the previous evening at the camp before taking off as a group for a weekend of camping at Lake Chala, about three hours south of TDC on the Kenya–Tanzania border. These young people were quite comfortable at TDC, having spent two weeks at the site during their orientation before moving into the communities. The night they were with us was much more active than most other nights, and they played guitar, sang, and generally had a good time. Amy was among the group and, as always, an active participant.

Halfway through our dinner, one of the ground staff approached our table and, in unfaltering Kiswahili, began talking to the Kenyan staff around the table. He grabbed the immediate attention of all of us. Although three of us understood little of what was being said, the wide eyes and open jaws of others at the table told the story very well.

It seemed that two of the TDC staff had overheard a radio communication between the police in the town of Taveta, where the student volunteers had gone, and those in Voi, the town closest to TDC, about fifty kilometers away. The report said that one person in a group of British young people was missing in the waters of Lake Chala. This was all that was relayed—no name, no details, and no way to verify the message because the transmitter was broken and we had no way to join the conversation. At TDC, our only real means of communicating with anyone more than twenty kilometers away was a satellite telephone that, throughout the evening, proved to be somewhat inefficient, occasionally losing its connection, delaying its message, and losing contacts.

We were left only imagining what might have happened. Hamisi, who was familiar with the area, having grown up nearby, thought that perhaps some of the students may have gone out in a dugout canoe with a local fisherman that then capsized. He quietly mentioned that there were crocodiles in the lake. After we spent two hours trying to obtain any information from local police headquarters and the Kenyan Tourist Commission in Nairobi, three vehicles left TDC to travel to Lake Chala. The time was 10:00 P.M.

The plan was to have two vehicles bring the young people back to TDC while one stayed behind to work with the local authorities. I was initially invited to accompany this group to serve as counselor to the young people on the ride back home, but this was changed at the last minute due to possible security threats and problems that might be encountered along the road, caused either by the common *shiftas*, or bandits, that frequently attacked vehicles at night, or by local authorities questioning a convoy of Kenyans with an American among the group. I waited the night for the group, and their story, to return. Remembering my experience as a young child at a summer camp when a drowning occurred, and the lack of recognition of my needs on the part of any adult, I decided that the least I could do was to be available to anyone who needed a listening ear or a shoulder to cry upon when they returned. It was a long night for everyone.

Two vehicles returned about 10:00 A.M. the following morning, carrying fifteen exhausted and emotionally drained young people back to camp. After climbing out of the vehicles, they dragged themselves, and their gear, ever so slowly into a large sitting area near the front gate. Not a word was spoken for some time until I cautiously began probing with a few questions. Not knowing how to begin such a painful conversation, I first asked if they had found people willing to assist them. Very few, they said, disappointed with the lack of police response and assistance provided by locals as well as camp staff where they were staying.

I then invited anyone to relate the events of the previous evening. Slowly and quietly we began to understand the horror these young people had just experienced. To be honest, it sounded like a script from a bad B horror movie—but it was very real.

It was late in the day when they all arrived. A few from the group asked some locals if it was OK to swim in the lake. They were assured that it was, although they were told that the nearby hotel allowed swimming in its pool for thirty shillings a person (about forty cents). No warnings about potential danger were offered. After quickly setting up camp and gathering some firewood and water for cooking, half a dozen boys went swimming off a nearby rock. As the sun began to set, and as they began to feel a bit uncomfortable and nervous, they wisely got out of the water.

It was close to 7:00 P.M. when three girls, including Amy, decided they would go in for a swim. Amy, you need to know, was an accomplished and confident swimmer, having worked as a lifeguard prior to coming to Kenya. The girls waded slowly along the shoreline, two of them up to their knees and Amy confidently moving out into chest-deep water. Suddenly, as the other two report, Amy was yanked underwater. The kids back at the camp, even those who were some distance from the water, all report hearing a scream but thinking that it was not much more than Amy seeing a snake along the shoreline. Amy remained underwater for about ten seconds before she reappeared, her head breaking the surface of the water only momentarily before she screamed, "A crocodile has me." She was violently thrust back underwater and pulled toward the right, not to be seen again. One boy, Andrew, who had witnessed all the activity from the shore, waded out with a flashlight in search of Amy. He reports seeing a couple of large eyes along the surface of the water not long after Amy disappeared. This was witnessed by at least three others at the scene.

Crocodiles are one of the most feared animals in all of Africa. They reportedly are man-eaters and, along with hippos and lions, account for more than a thousand deaths and disappearances a year. Several prey animals have been found wedged under submerged branches and stones, leading to reports that the crocodiles store unwanted prey until a later date. Some claim that this is necessary for the prey to decompose before the crocodiles are able to tear portions of flesh. When feeding, several crocodiles at a time will hold onto a carcass with their powerful jaws while twisting their bodies. The anchorage provided by the other animals allows large chunks to be torn off for easier swallowing. These are the gruesome details we were reading about as we pondered Amy's tragedy.

The young volunteers apparently pulled themselves together enough to begin a search-and-rescue mission, although they wisely did not reenter the water. They broke into three smaller groups: one searched along the shore of the lake; one tried, unsuccessfully, to get help from the local fishermen and hotel staff; and one group went out to the road hoping to locate the police. This went on until 3:00 A.M., when the group stopped searching, took three rooms at the hotel, and tried to get some rest.

As no telephone communication had been possible, they could only hope that staff at TDC would somehow find out about their plight and arrive. Knowing about the chances of meeting shiftas at night, they didn't expect that anyone from TDC would arrive until late the following morning, having waited until daybreak before taking to the roads. Exhausted, they were overjoyed when three TDC vehicles arrived at 4:00 A.M., thus relieving them of the pressures they were under to make decisions, attempt to take action, and deal with locals—all to no avail. Although happy to see staff from TDC, they were reluctant to leave without Amy.

The morning they returned was as somber as any that could be imagined. The group was given a decent meal and a chance to shower. Later they would meet with the Kenyan director of their program, who, along with the executive director from England who happened to be in the country, would charter a small plane and arrive by the end of the day, after making a brief visit to the scene of the incident. The kids were encouraged not to make any rash decisions, to pack all their belongings in case they decided against returning, and to plan to leave for Nairobi the following morning. They would stay in Nairobi for a week to gain some perspective, telephone their families, and then decide their future course of action. After two emotionally charged days with little, if any, sleep, they welcomed a night of rest. They spent the evening with their directors, sharing the experience as they remembered it, before turning in for the night.

As a father of a daughter just one month older than Amy, I was moved by the actions of these other young people. I was also encouraged by Amy's energy and eagerness to become active and involved in the lives of others. I cannot imagine the horror, however, of receiving a telephone call from overseas informing you that your daughter is missing and presumed dead—attacked by a crocodile, of all things.

Amy's father flew to Kenya the morning following the tragedy and immediately went on to Lake Chala. The Kenya Wildlife Service was on hand, organizing a search party of divers hoping to locate the body. Three days later, after the father had returned to Nairobi, the body was discovered, missing most of an arm. At least Amy's father had her body to take back home.

There is risk and danger in all we do, but we will never make this world a better place if we are not willing to take some risks, although guarded they must be. Most of the young people returned to their host communities and their volunteer work after a one-week stay in Nairobi. Their return to their villages demonstrated their commitment to the people with whom they had spent so much time. And although it must have been the most difficult of acts, Amy's parents have since donated the funds to build a community center in Bungule, Amy's village, in her memory.

Our relationship with the Kasigau teachers and community leaders has steadily evolved. Over a period of two years, I have arranged numerous trips to the region for faculty and teachers, offering workshops to local teachers, who typically receive little, if any, professional development once they are posted to the schools. And the level of trust has evolved to the point where we are able to engage local teachers, elders, and other community members in a curriculum project documenting the local way of life. We have trained local teachers in interview skills, and they are now documenting their own way of life for others to learn from and pass on to future generations.

11

MAKING IT WORK FOR YOU: TRAVEL TIPS AND RESOURCES

Now it's your turn. As you consider an overseas venture for yourself, your students, or your own children, there are a variety of sources that you can turn to for assistance. Following are an assortment of useful organizations, resources, and other considerations to help you make your trip planning and execution as rewarding and meaningful as possible. Go prepared, be safe, enjoy, and, most importantly, connect with and learn from others.

PREDEPARTURE TIPS

Teacher Tips

- Obtain required travel documents early in the trip planning. All travelers require a passport that officially identifies them as a citizen of a particular country. Passports, issued by the Department of State, are good for ten years (five years for people under eighteen years of age) and can be obtained at any U.S. Passport Agency or by mail at certain U.S. post offices that are designated to accept passport applications. Apply for passports as early as possible, as they can take between four to six weeks to process. Contact the

U.S. Department of State at its website at travel.state.gov/passport_services.html for comprehensive information and downloadable forms for applying for passports. Each applicant will require proof of citizenship (birth certificate or naturalization papers), two color passport photographs, proof of identity (driver's license with signature and photo), and an application fee. Passports must be valid for at least six months after the expected date of return, so keep them current.

- Certain countries require an official visa issued by their government that grants the traveler permission to enter the country. While many countries do not require Americans to obtain visas ahead of time (many countries, those in Western Europe for instance, issue them at the border as you enter the country), some do require advance processing. In such instances, the tour operator or travel agency will be able to advise. For non-Americans, different visa restrictions will apply, so consider such cases early in the planning.

- It is advisable to consider health and travel insurance early in program planning. In addition to having medical information on any student who has a medical history that may be of concern during the program, you should strongly recommend that each participant obtain health insurance that is fully applicable overseas in case of emergency. While you may have to pay for any medical emergencies out of pocket, having insurance will make it easier to obtain reimbursement upon return. Travel insurance is also advisable in case trip cancellation is necessary at the last minute for some unforeseen reason.

- Students of all ages might benefit from having an International Student Identity Card (ISIC). Recognized throughout much of the world, this card verifies student status, enabling card holders to obtain discounts from some airlines and insurance providers, as well as discounts or free admission to many museums and other cultural sites around the world. The ISIC also provides supplemental insurance coverage, including emergency medical evacuation in case of illness and repatriation in case of death—something most other policies do not include. The card is available at www.istc.org/sisp/index.htm?fx=istc_info.

Curricular-Related Issues

- The goals of cross-cultural training integrate nicely with the goals and objectives of good multicultural education programs. Look for ways to integrate these throughout your teaching.
- Good sources of both culture-specific and culture-general cross-cultural training materials are increasingly available from a variety of publishers. Try Intercultural Press (www.interculturalpress.com) for one of the most comprehensive collections of cross-cultural training materials. For a comprehensive academic treatment of intercultural training issues, see *Handbook of Intercultural Training*, available from Sage Publications (2nd edition, 1996, by Landis and Bhagat; 3rd edition, 2004, by Landis, Bennett, and Bennett).
- Visit the U.S. Department of State website for up-to-the-minute travel advisories as you plan to travel to any destination: www.state.gov/travel/.

Student Tips

- Make friends with people from as many different backgrounds as you can. This will help you learn to be comfortable with a wide range of cultural differences.
- When you find yourself judging others in a negative way, stop and ask yourself why they may be behaving in the manner that you are observing. Don't be afraid to ask others about the reasons they think and do things in particular ways.
- Expect there to be differences in such things as foods, weather, daily schedule, and supervision. At times, your teachers and chaperones will demand certain behavior or patience from you. Understand that while your group is traveling, the demands on everyone will be different. Some of these differences will be due to cultural differences, while others may be dictated by the fact that you are traveling in a group. The more flexible you can be, the easier will be your overall adjustment.
- Be aware and understanding of your own as well as your fellow students' feelings before and during travel. Some may find certain aspects of travel adjustments more difficult than others to adjust to at certain times and in certain circumstances. Some may be

surprised that they become homesick or have difficulties that they did not anticipate.

Parent Tips

- Retain a photocopy of your son or daughter's passport on file at home in case it is lost during travel.
- Help your children experience other cultural settings so they become comfortable and less judgmental about others. Visit other communities and religious settings, and vacation with this in mind.
- Encourage children to study a foreign language as early as possible in their schooling.
- People who tend to be effective in intercultural settings are eager to try new foods. Help children develop this eagerness by taking them to ethnic restaurants on a regular basis.
- Travelers should not carry large amounts of cash, and you are advised to consider currency needs prior to departure. Traveler's checks (in small denominations) and ATM cards (for most destinations) are the safest ways to obtain local currency. Each student should also have a small amount of local currency prior to leaving the airport. This can be obtained from most banks at home a few weeks before departure or at the airport, hotel, or bank upon arrival.
- Each individual has certain needs and desires as he or she travels that may need to be tempered or postponed in lieu of those of the group. Talk seriously with your son or daughter about the necessity to be flexible and cooperative during group travel.

TIPS WHILE TRAVELING

Teacher Tips

- The Council on Standards for International Educational Travel (CSIET) publishes a directory of international exchange programs that have been evaluated and found to be in compliance with CSIET standards. Schools can use their Model School Policy on International Student Exchange to assist them in administering successful international exchange programs. Obtain a copy through

CSIET, 212 South Henry Street, First Floor, Alexandria, VA 22314, or at www.csiet.org.
- Once you arrive in your country of destination, immigration officials will ask to see all passports and any necessary visas and will inquire about the purpose and length of stay in their country. Be sure all students have basic information about where they will be staying and for how long they will remain in the country. You may have to assist students in completing any arrival paperwork before they can proceed to claim their luggage.
- After passport control or immigration, and upon collecting your luggage, you will be asked to declare if you are carrying certain items with you (large sums of money, any restricted agricultural items, cameras and computers, and so forth). Luggage may also be opened and checked by government officials. Be certain that students take this exercise seriously, as the local officials certainly do. Discourage any wisecracks or joking about anything, especially bombs or illegal drugs.
- For the first few days after arrival, you and your students may experience jet lag. Jet lag is nothing more than your body clock trying to synchronize itself with the local time zone. Do not be surprised if people feel disoriented, wake up in the middle of the night, or fall asleep in the midafternoon for a few days. While jet lag is an inevitable part of travel, it can be minimized by avoiding alcohol and caffeine while traveling, setting your watch to the local time as soon as you depart, and adopting the local meal schedule as soon as possible.
- Soon after arrival you will want to do an on-site orientation to familiarize participants with specifics of the local program, including rules and any local laws students may not be familiar with. Any special health or safety precautions should be covered at this time, as well as culturally appropriate behavior people should be certain to adopt. Any basic language training might also begin at this time.
- You may want to encourage participants to communicate with home soon after arrival so people do not worry in these early days of the experience.
- You should register with any local authorities that are required, as well as the embassy of your country so you can be located in case of an emergency.

- Take time each day to help students reflect upon what they are experiencing. Focus special attention to cultural differences—the way people communicate with one another; the things that seem important in conversation, in the news, and on the streets. If staying with host families, what differences are students beginning to notice in the manner in which adults interact with children or the expectations parents have of children? If in schools, what differences stand out in the way teachers teach, in the interactions between teacher and student, or in the general behavior of students?

Student Tips

- It is in the early stages of a travel experience that you can begin to "learn how to learn." That is, adjusting to the local culture requires new sets of skills that you may not have used for some time. In the early days of your experience you will probably be excited. After some time, however, the excitement may wear off and be replaced by frustration as things you encounter on a regular basis may be quite different. Learn as much as possible from locals, keep your eyes and ears open, and ask as many questions of others as you can. If you have some basic cross-cultural concepts (e.g., the eighteen-theme culture-general framework), pay particular attention to these aspects. You can use these themes as starting points to begin to ask specific questions about how things are done locally.
- Keep a daily journal of your experiences. What have you observed? Who have you met? What significant differences seem to stand out to you? What questions do you have? How can you find out the answers to your questions?
- If you plan to be in the country for some time, keep your long-range goals in mind. Early on, you may be afforded special status as an outsider. People will be interested in you. Eventually, you will want to fit in like the locals, and others will begin to expect certain "local" behavior from you. Most locals have stereotypical images of Americans (or wherever you are from), based upon what they see in popular media and culture. Remember that you are an individual and work to dispel the stereotypes people may have of you. You can become an effective culture teacher in this regard.

- Do you want to get to know more locals? If you are staying with a family, or if you have access to a local home, offer to make a favorite meal for your hosts. This is a wonderful way of involving yourself with locals in a meaningful way. Or offer to make presentations at local schools and community organizations.
- Women traveling in some countries may wish to be especially cautious. Appropriate behavior for young women varies from country to country, and some nations have strictly defined gender roles. While it may be uncomfortable, learn how local women are expected to act and dress and try to behave accordingly. You may wish to dress modestly to reduce the likelihood of any unwanted sexual advances. Likewise, in some countries, girls' and young women's behavior may be more controlled by the family—and this includes host families. You may be expected to conform as anyone else in your family might. Try to view this as a compliment and a sign that you are being accepted as a local.
- Find out if there are any restrictions on eating or drinking to which you should be attentive. Find out if the local tap water is good to drink. Ask if you need to be certain to wash, peel, or boil fresh fruits and vegetables. While your stomach will take some time to adjust to local foods wherever you may be, there may be certain things you want to avoid.
- Do not be surprised if you experience diarrhea early in your trip. This is the most common form of traveler's illness and it will be almost impossible to avoid. In most cases it should only last a few days. During this time, be sure to replace lost fluids, eat carefully, and use medications wisely. If it lasts more than four or five days, or if it is accompanied by extreme pain, see a physician.
- Remember, ignorance of the law is no excuse. You are subject to all local laws and regulations, and your own government officials will not be able to intervene should you break the law. Be knowledgeable and wise.
- In some countries you will be perceived as rich and seen as an easy target, simply by the very nature of who you are. Think safety when you are out, especially at night. Use common sense: don't walk alone at night; don't wear expensive jewelry or flash expensive cameras; be cautious of road rules when walking or jogging;

find out from locals how to best use taxis and public transportation; know where high crime areas are and avoid them; and avoid large crowds that are big draws for pickpockets. And protect your passport at all times.

Parent Tips

- The Council on Standards for International Educational Travel (CSIET) publishes a directory of international exchange programs that have been evaluated and found to be in compliance with CSIET standards. Parents can use this as a guide to determine which international student exchange programs meet their children's needs and have met CSIET's high standards. Obtain a copy through CSIET, 212 South Henry Street, First Floor, Alexandria, VA 22314, or at www.csiet.org.

TIPS UPON RETURN

Teacher Tips

- When you and your students return home you will have to clear local customs and will again be asked to declare the value of any items purchased abroad. At the time of this writing, each returning American is allowed up to $400 in gifts and souvenirs without having to pay any tax or duty. There is generally a 10 percent tax on purchases made between $400 and $1,400, and anything over that amount is subject to a different rate (see the U.S. Customs website at www.cbp.gov/xp/cgov/travel/).
- If you are enriched and invigorated by the international experience, consider teaching overseas yourself, if even for one year. More than 1,000 English-language schools exist overseas to serve the needs of Americans and others who wish to have an American-oriented education. Organizations such as International Schools Services (ISS) and the European Council for International Schools (ECIS) offer placement services to assist schools and teachers in making an appropriate match. Subscribe to the *International Educator*, available at www.tieonline.com, to learn

about international-school issues and to keep abreast of international teaching vacancies.
- The Department of Defense operates a number of schools to serve the needs of U.S. military who are stationed overseas. Contact the department at www.odedodea.edu/pers/ to learn about teaching opportunities.
- Resources about reentry: Wang, M. M. 1997. Re-entry and reverse culture shock. In *Improving intercultural interactions: Modules for cross-cultural training programs*, vol. 2, ed. K. Cushner and R. W. Brislin. Thousand Oaks, CA: Sage Publications.

Student Tips

- Expect your reentry to be a bit bumpy and begin preparing yourself long before you are on the way home. Participate in any reentry workshops that may be offered.
- Take your reentry slow. Do not expect to feel like yourself immediately. It may take time to go through your own reentry experience. Be patient, and learn throughout the process.
- Think of yourself as entering a new culture and, as you were advised in your initial entry, ask questions when you do not know what is going on.
- Sharing your international experiences with others is often a good way of helping yourself work through some of your own reentry issues. Seek out audiences that would welcome you to make a presentation about your experience, such as foreign language classrooms at school, elementary or middle school social studies or language classes, local civic groups (Rotary Clubs, Boy and Girl Scouts, etc.). You should also continue meeting and talking with others who were on your trip. Sharing your feelings and frustration with others, while seeking out ways to integrate your new knowledge and experience, is often a help.
- Ask your family and friends to keep your letters, e-mail, and postcards and use them to remember and reflect upon your experience at a later time.
- Become active with a local international student club, or encourage your family to host an international student for a semester or year.

- Retain your international contacts. Keep in contact with the friends and families you cared about overseas. Keep as current as you can with news and other events from the country you left. Online versions of many newspapers from around the world are available via the Internet.

Parent Tips

- Be patient with your son or daughter. Breakdowns in communication are often at the heart of reentry difficulties, so listen and try not to judge. Your son or daughter may be experiencing a multitude of conflicting feelings and does not mean to hurt your feelings.
- Help your son or daughter find others who have had similar experiences to be with. Encourage others to listen to your child's adventures and to help him or her discuss the significant things he or she experienced and explore how he or she may have changed.
- Don't take it personally if the returnee does not seem interested in some of the activities or people you think he or she should be, or if he or she does not seem thrilled with a meal or activity you have planned.
- Seek out ways that your family might become more engaged internationally. Consider hosting an international student or becoming active in international community events.

CONTACTS REFERENCED THROUGH THIS BOOK

You can contact sites referenced in this book at the following:

Consortium for Overseas Student Teaching is able to make placements to member institutions only. See the consortium's website at www.teachabroad.ua.edu for additional information.

Legacy International Youth Program
1020 Legacy Drive
Bedford, VA 24523
website: www.legacyintl.org

Taita Discovery Centre
P.O. Box 630
Voi, Kenya
e-mail: discoverycentre@originsafaris.info

BOOKS AND ARTICLES OF INTEREST

Albert, R. D. 1986. Conceptual framework for the development and evaluation of cross-cultural orientation programs. *International Journal of Intercultural Relations* 10 (2): 197–213.

Bennett, M. J. 1993. Towards ethnorelativism: A developmental model of intercultural sensitivity. In *Education for the intercultural experience*, 2nd ed., ed. R. M. Paige. Yarmouth, ME: Intercultural Press.

Bhawuk, D. P. S. 2001. Evolution of culture assimilators: Toward theory-based assimilators. *International Journal of Intercultural Relations* 25 (2): 141–63.

Bhawuk, D. P. S., and R. W. Brislin. 2000. Cross-cultural training: A review. *Applied Psychology: An International Review* 49 (1): 162–91.

Brislin, R. W., K. Cushner, C. Cherrie, and M. Yong. 1986. *Intercultural interactions: A practical guide*, 1st ed. Beverly Hills, CA: Sage Publications.

Brislin, R. W., and P. B. Pedersen. 1976. *Cross-cultural orientation programs*. New York: Wiley.

Brislin, R. W., and T. Yoshida. 1994. *Intercultural communication training: An introduction*. Thousand Oaks, CA: Sage Publications.

———, eds. 1994. *Improving intercultural interactions: Modules for cross-cultural training programs*, vol. 3. Thousand Oaks, CA: Sage Publications.

Cushner, K. 1989. Assessing the impact of a culture-general assimilator. *International Journal of Intercultural Relations* 13 (2): 125–46.

———. 2003. *Human diversity in Action: Developing multicultural competencies for the classroom*, 2nd ed. Boston: McGraw-Hill.

Cushner, K., and R. W. Brislin. 1996. *Intercultural interactions: A practical guide*, 2nd ed. Thousand Oaks, CA: Sage Publications.

———, eds. 1997. *Improving intercultural interactions: Modules for cross-cultural training programs*, vol. 8. Thousand Oaks, CA: Sage Publications.

Fantini, A. E. 1991. Becoming better global citizens: The promise of intercultural competence. *Adult Learning* 2 (5): 15–19.

Fowler, S. M., and M. G. Mumford, eds. 1995. *Intercultural sourcebook: Cross-cultural training methods*, vol. 1. Yarmouth, ME: Intercultural Press.

———. 1998. *Intercultural sourcebook: Cross-cultural training methods*, vol. 2. Yarmouth, ME: Intercultural Press.
Gochenor, T., ed. 1993. *Beyond experience: The experiential approach to cross-cultural education*, rev. 2nd. ed. Yarmouth, ME: Intercultural Press.
Grove, C. L. 1989. *Orientation handbook for youth exchange programs*. Yarmouth, ME: Intercultural Press.
Grove, C. L., and I. Torbiörn. 1985. A new conceptualization of intercultural adjustment and the goals of training. *International Journal of Intercultural Relations* 9 (2): 205–33.
Hansel, B. 1993. *The exchange student survival kit*. Yarmouth, ME: Intercultural Press.
Hofstede, G. J., P. B. Pedersen, and G. Hofstede. 2002. *Exploring culture: Exercises, stories, and synthetic cultures*. Yarmouth, ME: Intercultural Press.
King, N., and K. Huff. 1985. *Host family survival kit: A guide for American host families*. Yarmouth, ME: Intercultural Press.
Kohls, L. R. 2001. *Survival kit for overseas living: For Americans planning to live and work abroad*, 4th ed. Yarmouth, ME: Intercultural Press.
Kohls, L. R., and J. M. Knight. 1994. *Developing intercultural awareness: A cross-cultural training handbook*, 2nd ed. Yarmouth, ME: Intercultural Press.
Landis, D., J. Bennett, and M. Bennett. 2004. *Handbook of intercultural training*, 3rd ed. Thousand Oaks, CA: Sage Publications.
Landis, D., and R. S. Bhagat, eds. 1996. *Handbook of intercultural training*, 2nd ed. Thousand Oaks, CA: Sage Publications.
Paige, R. M., ed. 1993. *Education for the intercultural experience*, 2nd ed. Yarmouth, ME: Intercultural Press.
Paige, M., A. Cohen, B. Kappler, J. Chi, and J. Lassegard. 2002. *Maximizing study abroad: A student's guide to strategies for language and culture learning and use*. Minneapolis: University of Minnesota, Center for Advanced Research on Language Acquisition.
Schmitz, J. 2000. *Cultural orientations guide: Building cross-cultural effectiveness*, 2nd ed. Princeton, NJ: Princeton Training Press.
Seelye, H. N., ed. 1996. *Experiential activities for intercultural learning*, vol. 1. Yarmouth, ME: Intercultural Press.
Spencer, S., and K. Tuma. 2002. *The guide to successful short-term programs abroad*. Washington, D.C.: NAFSA.
Storti, C. 1997. *Culture matters: The Peace Corps cross-cultural workbook*. Washington, D.C.: Peace Corps Information Collection and Exchange.
———. 1999. *Figuring foreigners out: A practical guide*. Yarmouth, ME: Intercultural Press.

———. 2001. *The art of coming home*. Yarmouth, ME: Intercultural Press.
———. 2001. *The art of crossing cultures*, 2nd ed. Yarmouth, ME: Intercultural Press.

CROSS-CULTURAL SIMULATIONS AND ACTIVITIES

Bafa Bafa: A cross-culture simulation. Available from Simulation Training Systems, Del Mar, CA. Rafa Rafa (the children's version) is also available.
Barnga: A simulation game on cultural clashes. Available from Intercultural Press.
Ecotonos: A multicultural problem-solving simulation, 2nd ed. Nipporica Associates and Dianne Hofner Saphiere. Available from Intercultural Press.
Global Awareness Profile (GAPtest). Available from Intercultural Press.
Randomia Balloon Factory. A unique simulation for working across the cultural divide. Available from Intercultural Press.

REFERENCES

Allport, G. 1954. *The nature of prejudice.* Reading, MA: Addison-Wesley.

Amir, Y. 1969. Contact hypothesis in ethnic relation. *Psychological Bulletin* 71 (5): 319–43.

Austin, C. 1986. *Cross-cultural re-entry: A book of readings.* Abilene, TX: Abilene Christian University Press.

Bennett, M. 1993. Towards ethnorelativism: A developmental model of intercultural sensitivity. In *Cross-cultural orientation*, ed. M. Paige, 27–69. Lanham, MD: University Press of America.

Brislin, R. W., K. Cushner, C. Cherrie, and M. Yong. 1986. *Intercultural interactions: A practical guide.* Thousand Oaks, CA: Sage Publications.

Chatwin, B. 1987. *The songlines.* New York: Penguin Books.

Cosineau, P. 1998. *The art of pilgrimage.* Berkeley, CA: Conari Press.

Cushner, K., and R. W. Brislin. 1996. *Intercultural interactions: A practical guide*, 2nd ed. Thousand Oaks, CA: Sage Publications.

Cushner, K., and A. Karim. 2004. Study abroad at the university level. In *Handbook of intercultural training*, 3rd ed., ed. D. Landis, J. Bennett, and M. Bennett. Thousand Oaks, CA: Sage Publications.

Cushner, K., and D. Landis. 1996. The intercultural sensitizer. In *Handbook of intercultural training*, 2nd ed., ed. D. Landis and R. Bhagat. Thousand Oaks, CA: Sage Publications.

Cushner, K., and J. Mahon. 2002. Overseas student teaching: Affecting personal, professional, and global competencies in an age of globalization. *Journal of Studies in International Education* 6 (1): 44–58.

Cushner, K., A. McClelland, and P. Safford. 2003. *Human diversity in education: An integrative approach*, 4th ed. Boston: McGraw-Hill.

DuBois, W. E. B. 1989. *The souls of black folks*. New York: Bantam Books.

Fussell, P. 1987. *The Norton Book of Travel*. New York: Norton.

Gmelch, G. 1997. Crossing cultures: Student travel and personal development. *International Journal of Intercultural Relations* 21 (4): 475–90.

Gullahorn, J. T., and J. E. Gullahorn. 1963. An extension of the U-curve hypothesis. *Journal of Social Issues* 19: 33–47.

Lemonick, M. 2000. Ancient exodus: Two skulls help explain when and why our ancestors left Africa. *Time*, May 22, 2000, 62.

Li, Y. 2000. Geographical consciousness and tourism experience. *Annals of Tourism Research: A Social Science Journal* 27 (4): 863–83.

Lysgaard, S. 1955. Adjustment in a foreign society: Norwegian Fulbright grantees visiting the United States. *International Social Science Bulletin* 7: 45–51.

Mahon, J. 2002. Intercultural sensitivity development among practicing teachers: Life history perspectives. Diss., Kent State Univ.

Mahon, J., and K. Cushner. 2002. The overseas student teaching experience: Creating optimal culture learning. *Multicultural Perspectives* 4 (3): 3–8.

Martin, J., and Harrell, T. 2004. Intercultural reentry of students and professionals. In *Handbook of intercultural training*, 3rd ed., ed. D. Landis, J. Bennett, and M. Bennett. Thousand Oaks, CA: Sage Publications.

Merryfield, M. M. 2000. Why aren't teachers being prepared to teach for diversity, equity and global interconnectedness? A study of lived experiences in the making of multicultural and global educators. *Teaching and Teacher Education* 16: 429–43.

Oberg, K. 1960. Culture shock: Adjustment to new cultural environments. *Practical Anthropology* 7: 177–82.

Pearce, R. H. 1965. *The savages of America: A study of the Indian and the idea of civilization*. Baltimore: Johns Hopkins University Press.

Pedersen, P. 1995. *The five stages of culture shock: Critical incidents around the world*. Westport, CT: Greenwood Press.

Pettigrew, T. 2001. Does intergroup contact reduce racial and ethnic prejudice throughout the world? Paper presented at the Second Biennial Meeting of the International Academy of Intercultural Research, Oxford, MS, April 21.

Piaget, J., and B. Inhelder. 1958. *The growth of logical thinking from childhood to adolescence*. New York: Basic Books.

Putnam, R. T., and H. Borko. 2000. What do new views of knowledge and thinking have to say about research on teacher learning? *Educational Researcher* 29 (1): 4–16.

REFERENCES

Quinn, D. 1995. *Ishmael: An adventure of the mind and spirit*. New York: Bantam Doubleday Books.

Sherif, M. 1958. Superordinate goals in the reduction of intergroup tensions. *American Journal of Sociology* 63 (4): 349–56.

Sikkema, M., and A. Niyekawa. 1987. *Design for cross-cultural living*. Yarmouth, ME: Intercultural Press.

Stephan, W. G. 1999. *Reducing prejudice and stereotyping in schools*. New York: Teachers College Press.

Stephan, W. G., and W. P. Vogt. 2004. *Learning to live together: Intergroup relations programs*. New York: Teachers College Press.

Triandis, H. 1972. *The analysis of subjective culture*. New York: Wiley Interscience.

Trifonovitch, G. 1977. Culture learning—culture teaching. *Educational Perspectives* 16 (4): 18–22.

Wang, M. M. 1997. Re-entry and reverse culture shock. In *Improving intercultural interactions: Modules for cross-cultural training programs*, vol. 2, ed. K. Cushner and R. W. Brislin. Thousand Oaks, CA: Sage Publications.

Ward, C., S. Bochner, and A. Furnham. 2001. *The psychology of culture shock*, 2nd ed. East Sussex: Routledge.

Wilson, A. 1987. Cross-cultural experiential learning for teachers. *Theory into Practice* 26: 519–27.

Zimpher, N. L. 1989. The RATE project: A profile of teacher education students. *Journal of Teacher Education* 40 (6): 27–30.

INDEX

adjustment, 41, 42, 62–64
adolescent exchange programs, 61–79, 148–49, 152
ambiguity, 33, 67, 69, 74
anxiety, 25, 31, 33, 34, 42–43, 67, 92, 93
arrival, 66–71, 149–52
attributions, 16, 52
Australia, 101–2, 103

Belize, 17–19, 20–22, 37–39, 41–44

categorization, 15, 55. See also stereotypes
change, resistance to, 51
cognitive complexity, 52, 53, 55
cross-cultural communication, 23
cross-cultural orientation. See orientation
cross-cultural training, 22–25, 29–31, 32–33, 147. See also orientation
culture assimilator, 32–33, 40. See also intercultural sensitizer

culture-general assimilator, 32–33, 40
culture-general training, 23, 32
culture learning, 16–17, 23, 39, 41, 51, 63, 72, 75–76, 106–9, 116, 117–21
culture shock, 27, 31, 43, 66, 71–75, 105–6
culture-specific training, 23, 32

Developmental Model of Intercultural Sensitivity (DMIS): acceptance, 57–58; adaptation, 58; defense, 56; denial, 54–55; integration, 58–59; minimization, 56–57
disconfirmed expectation, 15, 19–20, 23, 29, 66, 67, 70–71, 78, 118

emotional responses, 27, 29, 66, 67, 71–72, 98, 120
environmental conservation, 127–30, 137
ethnocentrism, 14, 16, 17, 23, 50–51, 52, 53–57, 63

ethnorelative orientation, 50, 52, 53, 57–59
experiential learning, 23, 50, 53, 109, 116–21

flexibility, 25
food safety, 25, 30–31, 151

generalizations, 55
global connectedness, 2–3, 5, 44
global education, 3, 23
Greece, 8–12
greeting behavior, 67–70
group travel. *See* travel

homesickness, 31, 43

iceberg analogy of culture, 40
illness, 151
impact of travel, 43–44, 45, 48–49, 79, 101–9, 111–21
integration, 58–59
intercultural competence, 23, 52, 59
intercultural development, 3–4, 51–59
intercultural sensitivity, 53–59, 62
intercultural sensitizer, 32–33, 40
intergroup relations, 87–91
international student teaching, 99–109
isomorphic attributions, 69
Israel, 81–84, 86–87, 91–98

jet lag, 149

Kenya, 45–49, 124–44
Kiswahili language, 1–2, 126

Legacy International Youth Program, 85–98

Mexico, 27–31, 33–35, 58
Middle East dialogue, 81–87, 91–98
multicultural education, 23, 107, 147

Neve Shalom, 83
New Zealand, 107

nonverbal communication, 70, 72, 74–75

objective culture, 39–41, 56, 62, 67, 93
orientation, 14–17, 22–25, 27, 29–31, 32–33, 49–52, 64–66, 106, 108–9

perspective differences, 67–68
perspective shift, 48–49, 50, 58, 84, 86, 103–5, 106
predeparture preparation, 64–66, 145–48
prejudice, 23

reentry, 64, 76–79, 111–12, 152–54
roles, 33, 76

safety concerns, 25, 151–52
second language learning, 24, 29, 72–74, 104
South Africa, 105–6, 108
State Department. *See* U.S. Department of State
stereotypes, 54–55, 82, 91, 98
study abroad, 113–16
subjective culture, 39–41, 42, 62, 93
summer youth programs, 81–98

Taita Discovery Centre, 124, 127–30, 137, 140–43
time orientation, 33–34, 138
travel: defined, 4; group travel, 39, 115, 119; reasons for, 4–8
trip development, 20–22
trust, 21, 72, 75, 83–84, 85–86, 88, 92, 125, 130, 133, 136

U.S. Department of State, 25, 145–46, 147
U-curve hypothesis, 62–63

W hypothesis, 63–64
women and travel, special concerns, 151

ABOUT THE AUTHOR

Kenneth Cushner, Ed.D., is executive director for international affairs and professor of education at Kent State University. He is a frequent contributor to the professional development of educators through consulting, writing, workshops, and travel programming. Ken is author or coauthor of numerous books and articles in this field, including *Human Diversity in Education: An Integrative Approach*, 4th ed., and *Intercultural Interactions: A Practical Guide*, 2nd ed. He has traveled with educators on all seven continents, and in his spare time he enjoys playing music (percussion and guitar), photography, and cycling.